RED REBEL

Tito of Yugoslavia

Dedicated revolutionary, heroic guerrilla commander and shrewd master of politics, Josip Broz Tito of Yugoslavia has left an indelible imprint upon the history of our times. Poverty and injustice made the young Tito receptive to the promises of Communism, and he participated in the Russian Revolution. For the next two decades he faced danger and imprisonment as he sought to bring that revolution to his native land. Then, in 1941, he led an ill-fed, ill-equipped Partisan army against the awesome Nazi military machine. By the war's end, Tito had become the undisputed leader of his people—and had come to the painful realization that what was good for Russia was not automatically good for Yugoslavia. Tito's daring break with Stalin, and his insistence upon Yugoslavia's right to follow an independent road to Socialism, dealt the solidarity of the Communist camp a blow from which it has never fully recovered, and taught the West to avoid the mistake of assuming that all Communist nations were alike.

Books by Jules Archer

RED REBEL
Tito of Yugoslavia

SCIENCE EXPLORER
Roy Chapman Andrews

WORLD CITIZEN
Woodrow Wilson

BATTLEFIELD PRESIDENT
Dwight D. Eisenhower

FIGHTING JOURNALIST
Horace Greeley

MAN OF STEEL
Joseph Stalin

TWENTIETH-CENTURY CAESAR
Benito Mussolini

FRONT-LINE GENERAL
Douglas MacArthur

RED
REBEL

Tito of Yugoslavia

by Jules Archer

JULIAN MESSNER **New York**

Published simultaneously in the United States and Canada by Julian
Messner, a division of Simon & Schuster, Inc., 1 West 39 Street, New York,
N.Y. 10018. All rights reserved.

Printed in the United States of America
Library of Congress Card No.: 68–25097

Contents

To
Phil Hirsch

who first encouraged me to write the remarkable
story of the maverick Marshal of the Balkans

Foreword

It would be difficult to overestimate the impact Marshal
Josip Broz Tito of Yugoslavia has had upon the twentieth
century. Until his emergence on the world stage after World
War II, nations under Communism were a monolithic structure dominated by Moscow. Tito's defiance of Joseph Stalin,
his insistence upon Yugoslavia's right to follow an independent road to Socialism, shook the world of Communism
to its foundations.

It led to revolts in eastern Europe, and contributed to
the split between the Soviet Union and Red China. Tito
taught the West to avoid the mistake of assuming that *all*
Communist nations were alike. And he brought about a
third bloc of neutral nations to stand between the two great
powers—the US and the USSR—as a balancing force.

This book is addressed to the American citizens and
statesmen of tomorrow, who will need a clear, cool, fresh
approach to the question of world Communism and how to
deal with it intelligently. Nuclear weapons have made a
purely military response to Communism obsolete as a foreign policy. Most people of the West recognize that if we
and the Communist nations do not learn to live together,
we may die together.

Any military victory we achieve would scarcely be
worth it if we blow up the world and ourselves in the
process. It would seem more sensible to search for new
policies that preserve the principles of Western democracy
without violating world peace. Tito has insisted that internal differences of government systems need not prevent

7

Communist and non-Communist countries from sharing the globe peacefully.

The eminent British historian Professor Arnold Toynbee declares that only Americans today still believe in the theory that Communist nations act together in a giant conspiracy against the West. "Every Communist country and every capitalist country is a nationalist country first," he points out. "Yugoslavia, Russia, North Vietnam, South Vietnam's Vietcong, China, Outer Mongolia—they are all Communist, but they are nationalist first."

In today's complex world we need a realistic, sophisticated view of world affairs and of controversial world figures like Marshal Tito of Yugoslavia. Studying the story of Tito, we can understand not only the weaknesses of Communism but also its nationalistic appeal to the people of countries who have suffered severely under misrule by local despots or alien colonialists.

This knowledge can help us learn how to compete effectively with Communists for the hearts and minds of people in the underdeveloped nations of Asia, South America and Africa. Tito is an ideal object for this study because he represents successful Communist leadership at its most beguiling.

Dr. Richard P. McCormick, professor of history at Rutgers University, warned in a report to the American Historical Association that too many history books are more intent upon creating an artificial jingoistic patriotism, often a naked nationalism, than upon the accurate teaching of history.

"It is not necessary to make a heel of George III," Dr. McCormick pointed out, "in order to make a hero of George Washington. . . . There is enough misunderstanding abroad in the world; we should avoid teaching misunderstanding in our schools." I have tried to follow this advice.

This book attempts neither to vilify nor to glorify Josip

Broz Tito, but to tell his story as honestly as the evidence allows. All possible sources of information on his life were consulted—those portraying him as the devil incarnate; those glorifying him as a modern-day Robin Hood; those sincerely trying to be objective. The Yugoslav government was informed of the project and told that it would be written impartially, with the subject's shortcomings as well as virtues candidly described.

Milos Nikolic, Public Relations Officer of the Yugoslav Information Center in New York City, cooperated by making available invaluable source material, for which the author wishes to express sincere appreciation. Neither Mr. Nikolic nor anyone connected with the Yugoslav government, however, has been given the opportunity to see this book before publication, so that full responsibility for all facts and opinions about Marshal Tito, favorable and unfavorable, rests upon the shoulders of the author alone.

Mr. Nikolic was queried as to whether it would be proper to use the Yugoslav spelling of names without the great variety of phonetic accent marks, in order to make them easier for Americans to read. He replied that most American books about Yugoslavia do eliminate these marks, although some do not. "The usage of alphabet and spelling," Mr. Nikolic advised, "depends upon the author." This book therefore uses the correct Yugoslav spelling of names without the phonetic symbols.

Jules Archer

Pine Plains
New York

RED REBEL
Tito of Yugoslavia

1

Prisoner-of-War

JOSIP BROZ, later to become famous as Tito, was born on May 25, 1892, in the picturesque Croat village of Kumrovec. As a boy he lived a rugged outdoor life in this Zagorje Mountain region of what was then part of the Austro-Hungarian Empire. Twenty miles to the south lay the Croat capital, Zagreb; 150 miles to the north, Vienna; 175 miles to the northeast, Budapest; 90 miles to the west, Trieste.

Josip's birthplace, a small pastel blue cottage with homemade roof tiles, overlooked a pretty valley through which the green Sutla River meandered. His father, Franyo Broz, was a Croat peasant. The Croats were a proud, rebellious race, speaking their own Slav tongue and clinging to ancient traditions, always a thorn to whatever power overran them.

Marija Broz, Josip's mother, was a tall, blonde, blue-eyed Slovene, a Roman Catholic like her husband. They had fifteen children; Josip was the seventh. But harsh mountain winters, hunger and privation took a severe toll of the Broz family. Eight of Josip's brothers and sisters died before outgrowing childhood.

Genial Franyo Broz, fonder of talking than tilling, was almost always in debt. He tried to augment his meager farm income with odd jobs as blacksmith, mineral-bath attendant and wood-hauler. But discouragement soon turned him to tippling at the inns, which saw more of him than his family did.

Working from dawn to dark and long after, keeping her children busy and out of trouble, Marija struggled valiantly to scrape up enough food daily for her big family. But times were lean and Josip often went to bed hungry.

They all lived in two rooms—half a tiny farmhouse shared with a family of cousins. The older children slept in an upstairs garret; Josip and the younger children bedded down on rags on the floor beside their parents' bed.

Each time one of his brothers or sisters died, Josip found himself baffled by the priest's explanation of "God's will." Why did God want his brothers and sisters to die? His early religious feeling as an acolyte in the village church was dampened by a gruff new priest who boxed Josip's ears for being clumsy in helping him off with his vestments. Josip's proud spirit rebelled when anyone laid a hand on him.

From the time he was seven he cheerfully carried water for the household, hoed corn, weeded the garden, turned the heavy grindstone that crushed grain into flour. He enjoyed working outdoors, tending the farm horses most of all.

"I rode bareback when my head barely reached the horse's belly," he recalled later fondly. Even at that age he loved horses so much that in riding them through the mountains, he would always dismount going uphill to ease their climb.

A two-room elementary school opened in 1899 with one teacher for Kumrovec's 350 children. Josip attended for four years, doing his homework in the meadow as he pastured the family cow. The teacher found him a courteous, bright boy with an inquisitive mind. Gymnastics, gardening and Scriptures were his best subjects. After school, chores done, Josip would go riding, or swim and fish in the Sutla, or climb up to play in the ruins of ancient Cesargrad Castle.

Likable, athletic, tough but fair, the wiry Josip was the popular choice to lead exciting raids on fruit orchards and battles against boys from the next village. His forays were marked by ingenious strategy and cool courage.

Once he was trapped in a pear tree by a widely feared orchard owner who threatened to beat him to a pulp when he came down. Josip solved the problem by dropping out of the tree on the farmer's head, flattening him, then scooping up a few pears as he made his escape. No raid was ever too daring, no mountain too steep, no bully too big, for Josip Broz.

Despite his talent for mischief, most adults in Kumrovec found his bright grin irresistible. As a child he was his mother's favorite. Seeing herself mirrored in his curly blond, blue-eyed good looks, she often yielded to his persistent demand for stories and songs. None loved Josip more than his mother's father. His Slovenian grandfather was a merry farmer who shared Josip's love of pranks. When Josip was allowed to stay with him, they would hike through the valley of the Sutla, the woods ringing with their laughter.

Other occasions that brightened Josip's poverty-ridden youth were the folk festivals. Everyone drank sugared *sljivovica,* and he would join in dancing the gay *kolo slavon* to accordion and violin, along with Kumrovec men in small brimless hats, linen trousers and big boots, and village women in flaring multiple skirts and richly embroidered blouses.

One of the saddest times for Josip was the bitter winter his father sold the family sheep dog, Polak, to buy firewood. Josip was heartbroken. Polak was one of the family; how could his father do such a thing? To his delight Polak suddenly showed up in their garden two days later, an obvious runaway from his new owner. Josip quickly smuggled him up to a mountain cave and kept him hidden there until he was sure that his new owner had abandoned the search for him.

When Josip was fourteen his father decided that he was old enough to leave home and support himself. "Get him a job as a waiter," a visiting relative advised. "A waiter is always well-dressed, always among nice people and gets plenty to eat without too much hard work." It was the thought of being able to dress well that appealed to the ragged peasant boy who seldom had enough warm clothes for the rugged Yugoslav winters. In the Zagorje, respect automatically went to anyone successful enough to afford unpatched coats or trousers.

His father found an apprentice waiter's job for him in Sisak, a town fifty miles southeast, and Josip left home for the first time in 1906. He was fascinated by his first glimpse of Croatia's "better classes"—urbane businessmen and polished army officers, and their elegantly dressed ladies.

Serving them under the trees of Sisak's leading café to the strains of a gypsy band, he marveled how different life here was from primitive Kumrovec. One day, he mused, perhaps he, too, would be able to live in such fine style. But he could hardly expect to get anywhere as long as he continued to wait on tables and wash dishes. He was also bored because, after the first few days, there had been nothing more to learn. Surely there was some other employment in Sisak that was more challenging, with more of a future!

One day, serving a cup of *turska kava* (Turkish coffee) to a good-natured local locksmith named Nicholas Karas, Josip pleaded for a chance to learn the metalworking trade. Karas agreed to take him on as an apprentice. An astute and skillful pupil, Josip delighted in the whir of lathes, the smell of molten metal, the flash of yellow sparks.

Karas fed him well, let him sleep in the shop with other apprentices, and sent him to school two evenings a week. The school library had more books than Josip had ever seen in his life, and he became an avid reader. Sometimes he devoured as many as six books a week on history, travel, adventure.

One day, shortly before his three-year apprenticeship was due to end, he became so absorbed in *The Adventures of Sherlock Holmes* that he could not bear to put it down when work began. Instead of watching his lathe drill, he continued reading surreptitiously. The drill suddenly snapped.

Outraged, Nicholas Karas lashed out with a powerful fist. Josip went flying. As he picked himself up off the floor, tears stung the eighteen-year-old boy's eyes. Always sensitive to physical punishment, his feelings hurt more than his jaw. He had deserved a reprimand, yes—but not such a humiliating attack on his personal dignity! The next morning he was gone.

It was a criminal offense to violate an apprenticeship contract, and Karas was legally required to report Josip's disappearance to the Sisak police. They located him in a nearby village, working at making bricks. Jailed, he brooded unhappily until Karas, who was not an unkind man, sent a warm dinner to his cell. Josip quickly accepted Karas' offer to take him back to complete his apprenticeship.

In 1910, Josip bid Karas a grateful good-bye and left for Zagreb. In the capital of Croatia, he joined the Metalworkers Union and found work as a mechanic. His informal education took a political turn when radical union members taught him to understand the unique problems of his native land—a Balkan peninsula standing at the crossroads where the forces of East and West met and clashed.

Josip learned how the provinces of the Croats and their neighbors—Serbs, Macedonians, Bosnians, Slovenes and

Montenegrins—had been laid waste in a power struggle
between the Austro-Hungarian Empire and the Ottoman
Turks. Their men, women and children had been put to
the sword until the charred earth was fertilized with their
blood.

Conflicting religions had also ripped the Slavic peoples
apart, setting Roman Catholic Croats and Slovenes against
Orthodox Serbs, Macedonians and Montenegrins, as well as
Moslem Bosnians against both sects. Each faction fought the
other fiercely and frequently, hating each other too much
to unite against enemy invaders of their land.

The answer, union radicals told young Josip, was a new
movement that would unite Slav workers and peasants
against the priests of *all* religions, against the big powers
that constantly overrun them, against the wealthy classes
who exploited their labor. That movement was called Socialism. Greatly impressed, Josip joined the Croat Social Democrat Party.

Severe unemployment sent him from city to city in
search of work. But even when he found it, a restless urge
to see the world kept him from staying long in one place.
His wanderings took him to Fiume, Vienna, Mannheim, Pil-
sen and Munich. Often finding himself without food or
shelter for the night, he simply went hungry and slept in
barns or fields. Travel strengthened his self-reliance, making
him stoically indifferent to hardships. It also fed his appetite
for learning.

In German railways and shipyards he studied engineering on the job. In Vienna he learned how to play chess, how
to waltz and how to speak German with a Viennese accent.
In Chenkov he mastered the Czech tongue, and perfected
his skill in gymnastics at the Sokol physical-culture center.
Working as a mechanic at the Daimler works outside of
Vienna, he studied Marx in German and learned how to test-
drive automobiles, despite an accident that scarred his right
hand.

For Josip Broz, at twenty-one, the day when he failed to learn something new was a wasted day. It was in this spirit that he accepted his call-up in 1913 for a required two years of military service in the Austro-Hungarian Army. His rugged upbringing in the Zagorje Mountains, his experience in roughing it around southern Europe and his gymnastic prowess, all combined to make him enjoy soldiering in the 25th Home Guard Regiment.

When he had completed one year of service, Josip's life was suddenly changed by a pistol in the hand of a young Serb terrorist, Gavrilo Princip, in Sarajevo, Bosnia. On June 28, 1914, Princip expressed Serb indignation over Austrian annexation of Bosnia by killing the visiting Hapsburg heir to the Austrian throne, Archduke Franz Ferdinand. Austria promptly declared war on Serbia, with German backing. To Serbia's defense rushed Russia, England, France and Italy. The great guns of World War I began to roar in August in a power clash between the Central Powers and the Allies.

Josip was sent to Budapest for training in a school for noncommissioned officers. Here his expert swordsmanship, athletic prowess and leadership ability won him assignment to a Croat artillery regiment as its sergeant major.

After some halfhearted battles against the Serbs near Belgrade, his regiment was ordered to the Carpathian front to meet the advancing Russians, then only 125 miles from Budapest. The winter was bitterly cold. Both sides, poorly equipped with thin shoddy uniforms and boots that melted in sleet and snow, suffered from frostbite.

At night, staring across snow-covered mountain slopes littered with moonlit dead bodies, Josip Broz found himself wondering why he should be shooting at Russian workers in uniform, and they at him. Both were Slavic peoples, weren't they? He expressed his doubts to a friend beside him in their front-line observation post.

"Maybe the Tsar and the Emperor of Austria-Hungary hate each other," he shrugged, "but what's that to do with us? I don't hate Ivan, and I'm sure he doesn't hate me. I think it would make more sense if we both just turned around and fired our weapons at our own officers instead."

"*Nemoguce!*" gasped the other man. "Impossible!"

An old sergeant major overhead them and reported Josip's unpatriotic remark to the commanding officer of the artillery regiment. Josip was arrested and put into a fortress jail on the Danube. At a hearing four days later his friend denied that he had ever made the seditious remark. The commandant chose to give Josip the benefit of the doubt, and sent him back to rejoin his regiment near Okna.

Despite his lack of enthusiasm for the war, Josip could not resist demonstrating his personal prowess as a soldier. He led raids behind enemy lines, enjoying the challenge and the danger, always displaying a cool courage and quick intelligence that made his men admire and trust him. They were also devoted to him for his warm interest in their families back home, as well as his stubborn insistence that they get the full rations, issues of new shoes and decent sleeping accommodations due them whenever these were available.

He never lacked for volunteers to follow him.

The company commander, Captain Tomasevic, still suspected him of disloyal feelings, but could not deny Josip's resourcefulness, courage and skill on reconnaissance. One night the tough scout and his men surprised eighty Russian soldiers asleep deep in enemy territory without guards posted. His men wanted to slaughter them, but Josip whispered, "Why such useless bloodshed? Let's bring them all back." So they did. The prisoners provided valuable military information.

But there was only one Josip Broz fighting against the Russians in the icy Carpathian Mountains. On Easter morning, 1915, the Austrian forces fell back in panic, abandoning Josip's regiment to the mercies of a massive Russian advance.

Fierce mounted Circassians surrounded the embattled Croats. Wielding iron-tipped, two-pronged lances, they swooped down from all sides at once.

Josip stood his ground, fighting furiously in a muddy trench as two Russians flung themselves upon him. While he struggled with one, the other drove a lance into his back, narrowingly missing his heart. He fell unconscious.

When he regained his senses, he found himself headed for Khirgisia in central Asia, a prisoner with other Croats of his regiment. Many had quickly surrendered to the Russians, relieved to be out of the war. Josip was also glad that he no longer had to fight against an enemy he did not really believe to be *his* enemy. Yet he was youthfully proud of the brave account he had given of himself as a soldier.

A monastery near Kazan, Russia, had been taken over as a prisoner-of-war hospital. It took a full year for Josip to recover from his wounds, complicated by typhus and pneumonia, but his rugged constitution pulled him through.

Characteristically, as soon as his fever subsided, he began to study Russian. Two local teen-age girls helped by sending books to the prisoners. Josip was soon reading Turgenev, Tolstoi, Gogol, Dostoyevsky and Gorky in the original Russian. Discovering these writers excited Josip as no books had ever done before. Their brilliant insights into human nature and the Russian character led him to believe that Russians were the most intelligent, decent and perceptive people on earth. He felt an egotistic thrill of identity.

After all, *he* was a Slav, too!

In his enthusiasm, the new Russophile did not pause to reflect that Russia had also produced an Ivan the Terrible, a Rasputin and other unsavory characters. When Lenin and Stalin appeared on the Russian stage, Josip was prepared to see in them only idealists like the great Russian writers he so admired. He took it for granted that the new Soviet society would reflect the humanity of the Russian classics.

His Russian captors treated him well, viewing him more as a fellow Slav than a prisoner-of-war. He was given a job as a mill mechanic, then promoted to supervision of a railway gang in the Urals. In his customary zeal to look out for his men, he angrily reported the chief of the railway section for stealing the prisoners' Red Cross parcels.

The furious chief waited for a chance for revenge. It came when Josip failed to report the late arrival at work of three of his men who had been in camp repairing their felt boots in order to be able to work in the snow. Three Cossacks flung him into jail and lashed him across the back with their knouts.

"I endured thirty blows," he recalled grimly, "that I shall remember all my life." But the jailer, a kindhearted and good-natured Russian, treated his wounds, gave him blankets and tea, and even soothed him by playing Russian folk songs on the balalaika.

It was March, 1917. Electrifying news came from Petrograd. The Tsar had abdicated, forced out by a Menshevik revolution. The new Kerensky regime ordered the release of all prisoners-of-war. Josip promptly hopped a grain freight train to Petrograd, where Socialism had come to power for the first time on earth. He was eager to be a part of it in some way.

But in Petrograd, taking part in demonstrations calling for Russia's withdrawal from the war, Josip fell in with members of the Bolshevik Party. They convinced him that Kerensky was not an apostle of true Socialism, but its betrayer. He joined them in agitating for the overthrow of the Menshevik regime in favor of a militant workers' government.

Kerensky ordered a crackdown on the Bolsheviks. Josip was one of those caught and imprisoned in the damp, rat-infested dungeons of the St. Peter Fortress. After three weeks he was put on a train bound for a Siberian prison camp.

En route in October, the train was halted at one station by exciting news. The Bolsheviks had chased Kerensky out of the Winter Palace in Petrograd, and the Communist Party had taken power. The train commander hesitated, perplexed as to whether to go on with his cargo of political prisoners or turn back. Eluding guards, Josip jumped off the train, sprinted across the tracks and leaped aboard a passenger train moving out of the station back to Petrograd.

He found the Bolsheviks busy organizing Red Guard units to hold key cities against counterattacks by anti-Communist White Russian forces. He joined one and was sent to Omsk. An attack by Admiral Kolchak's forces took the city, scattering its Red Guard defenders. Josip escaped by hiding out in the house of a Bolshevik sympathizer named Byelusnova.

One night his host's pretty seventeen-year-old daughter, Polga, helped Josip slip through White Russian lines, guiding him to the camp of a primitive, half-nomadic Mongol tribe in the nearby Steppes. "You will be safe here," she told him.

"I'll come back to you, Polga," he vowed. Like all decisions Josip Broz made, this one had been swift but certain. He was in love and intended to take a Russian bride.

2

"Arrest Josip Broz!"

Isaiah Djaksembayev, chief of the Kirghiz tribe, welcomed Josip with open arms. He badly needed a mechanic to operate a motorized flour mill the tribe had acquired. The newcomer, adaptable as ever, quickly accustomed himself to the rugged Kirghiz way of life. Djaksembayev was impressed and delighted when the Croat proved the equal of a Mongolian in horsemanship, spearing wolves in moonlight at full gallop and breaking wild horses.

The Kirghiz tested him with a stallion that had never felt a man on his back. The horse reared and pawed the air savagely, but Josip managed to saddle, bridle and mount him. The stallion galloped madly into the nearest woods to scrape the frightening burden off its back by racing beneath tree branches. Face and torso bloodied, Josip stayed in the saddle for half an hour until the chastened steed accepted defeat.

The Moslem chief embraced him in admiration.

Josip adopted their tribal dress and quickly mastered the Kirghiz tongue. He was enormously popular with the

24

Steppes nomads as they swapped lusty stories around the firelight. It was a wild, rough, romantic way of life, and he thoroughly enjoyed it.

But there was a world to be won. When the Bolsheviks finally retook Omsk, Josip said good-bye to Isaiah Djaksembayev, whose eyes brimmed with tears at losing him.

On the way back to Omsk a group of mounted bandits dashed across his path, flinging up rifles. "Don't shoot," Josip urged them. "I'm a prisoner-of-war from the Balkans." The bandits deliberated, stripped him of everything Djaksembayev had given him, then allowed him to proceed.

Returning to the Byelusnova house, Josip promptly asked Polga to marry him. Fascinated by the engaging smile and deep blue eyes of the sturdy blond Croat, she accepted. They were married in a brisk ceremony and left for Petrograd early in 1920. The Bolsheviks were now firmly in control of most parts of Russia. Josip was enthralled by the revolutionary changes he saw being made as a vast society transformed itself from a Tsarist empire to a land of Socialism.

Hearing that the political earthquake on the banks of the Neva had produced revolutionary tremors in his own country, Josip decided to go home. The small part he had played in the Bolshevik victory had taught him how to be a revolutionary; now he would fight for Communism in the Balkans.

The journey home by train and ship was long and arduous, especially for Polga, who was now expecting a child. At the Serbian border they were arrested as "Bolsheviks" because they were coming from Red Russia, but were released after a few days. Josip found the region he had called home recast in an entirely new framework as a result of the peace settlement at Versailles over a year earlier.

The Austro-Hungarian Empire was no more. Austria was now a shrunken mountain state surrounding Vienna.

Hungary was independent. The north of the Hapsburg Empire had been turned into the new nation of Czechoslovakia, uniting Czechs, Slovaks and Ruthenians. The south of the Empire had become Yugoslavia, embracing five million Serbs, three million Croats, a million Slovenes and three million assorted minorities, especially Macedonians, Bosnians and Montenegrins.

Schoolboys in the new state of Yugoslavia had begun to recite a new catechism called *What Is Yugoslavia?*: "There are six republics, five nations, four languages, three religions, two alphabets, but only one desire—independence!" Since the Serbs had fought on the winning side of the World War, and also constituted the largest single faction in the new country, they emerged in control of the first postwar government under King Alexander. The Croats and Slovenes resented legislation by the new Yugoslav Parliament, most of it favoring the Serbs at their expense.

Widespread unrest and dissatisfaction had resulted in the election of fifty-three Communists—one out of every eight deputies—to the Parliament. Bread was hard to find and expensive. Most goods could be bought only on the black market, at exorbitant prices. Nine out of ten industrial workers were unemployed, and strikes were spreading. Josip Broz was more convinced than ever that there was only one answer to the new country's problems: a Russian-type Socialism.

He returned to Kumrovec with Polga in September, 1920. Bursting through the front door of his family home to embrace his mother, he was bewildered to find only strange faces. His father, he learned, had moved to a neighboring village. Tears welled to his eyes when he was told that his mother had died two years earlier. With a heavy heart he made his way to his father's new home, to be greeted unenthusiastically.

"You might better have stayed in Russia," Franyo Broz

grunted. "Food is scarce here. The only place you're likely to find any work is in Zagreb."

Josip's jaw clenched. "Don't worry, Father, we'll leave as soon as the baby is born. It's just a matter of hours."

"Oh, you can stay a few days." Franyo dourly eyed the Red Guard sheepskin hat with red star that Josip had taken out of his baggage and proudly worn home. "But you'd better get rid of *that*. Unless you're looking for trouble!"

Only hours after their arrival Polga gave birth to a baby boy. But the rigors of the long, difficult journey from Petrograd had been too much. The baby died two days later.

They left for Zagreb, where Josip found a job as machinist in an engineering shop. Renewing his old membership in the Metalworkers Union, he also joined the Zagreb branch of the Yugoslav Communist Party. He enthusiastically agreed with their policy of first allegiance to the Soviet Union. The USSR was the only workers' government on earth, wasn't it? Well, then, whatever benefited the USSR had to benefit workers *everywhere,* advancing the cause of world revolution. Josip was especially welcome to the YCP as a Croat who had spent five years in Russia and taken part in the Soviet revolution. Like America's Lincoln Steffens, he declared enthusiastically, "I have seen the future, and it works!"

He organized a Red cell within the Metalworkers Union. His fellow workers were fond of him as a union brother who could crack jokes with them one moment, the next explain a fine point about local labor affairs or the Soviet Union. His readiness to go out of his way to do anyone a favor added to his popularity. The metalworkers responded unanimously to his call that winter for a strike in Zagreb.

The strike touched off a series of other industry shutdowns, with workers demanding better wages and working conditions. The Belgrade government, fearful of the spectre of revolution, cracked down severely. Josip was fired, the strikes crushed. In December, 1920, Police Minister Milorad Draskovic closed Communist Party headquarters, seized the Party newspaper and ordered an end to Red propaganda. The Communists struck back in the summer of 1921.

Draskovic was assassinated by a radical named Rodolyub Tsolakovic, who was caught and sent to prison. Josip viewed the assassination as a necessary act of class warfare, fully justified by the killing of striking workers by Draskovic's police. Terror had to be fought by counter-terror. Josip did not forget Rodolyub Tsolakovic, who spent a dozen years in prison. Following World War II, Tsolakovic was made President of the Bosnia-Herzegovina republic of a Red Yugoslavia.

But in 1921 the assassination provoked stern reprisals. The government declared the Communist Party illegal, and threw its fifty-nine elected deputies out of Parliament. Josip's comrades attempted to assassinate King Alexander but failed. He was forced to flee Zagreb along with them. "The Communist Party of Yugoslavia . . . was beheaded, even broken," he admitted.

With Polga he found refuge and a new job in the little Croatian village of Veliko Trojstvo. The elderly Jewish owner of a flour mill, Samuel Polak, hired him as a mechanic for the mill engine. Polak soon became aware that his new employee was making contact with underground Red cells, and was actively engaged with them in spreading revolutionary propaganda. He told Josip with a shrug, "You're a good mechanic, Broz. It's no concern of mine what you do outside the mill."

But an enraged local priest brought charges of subversion against Josip. Arrested, he was marched through the street in chains. After a week in jail he was brought to trial. But the prosecuting attorney, an Orthodox Church member who hated Roman Catholics, helped Josip win dismissal of the priest's charges. Josip was soon busy helping fellow radicals collect and conceal weapons in a secret dump outside the village, against the day of revolution.

The years he and Polga spent in Veliko Trojstvo were marked by personal sorrow. After having lost their firstborn, they had three more children, but one died after a few days and a second perished of diphtheria at the age of two. Only a fair-haired, blue-eyed son called Zarko survived.

The coffins for the dead Broz children were made by a cabinetmaker named Franjo Podupski, who sadly watched Josip carry them on his shoulder to the cemetery. "He was deeply moved," Podupski recalled years later. "It was the third child that had died. Such was the life of a worker. I never charged him anything for the coffins."

When police surveillance, alerted by his arrest, kept his movements under too close a scrutiny, Josip and his family slipped out of Veliko Trojstvo one night and made their way to the tiny Adriatic town of Kraljevica. Here they lived in a shack on a vine-covered cliff overlooking an azure Dalmatian bay. Josip found work as a shipyard mechanic.

His fellow workers had grievances of long standing against the company, and quickly responded when Josip organized a local of the Metalworkers Union. Elected shop steward, he called a strike. The union won most of its demands, but Josip was fired. He shrugged; there were always jobs for skilled mechanics. Before he left Kraljevica, he made sure the union was firmly controlled by a Communist Party cell. When the time was ripe, it would be the task of such cells to rally union workers to the revolutionary barricades.

Organizing and agitating from town to town, Josip was repeatedly fired as a troublemaker. Late in 1926 he was summoned to Moscow by the Comintern, the international league of Communist parties controlled by the Kremlin. Polga and Zarko went along to visit her parents. Seeing

Moscow for the first time—he had only been in Petrograd, the old Bolshevik capital—Josip stared around him with pride and awe. To think that this great city, this great nation, was now in the hands of Communist workers like himself! One day, hopefully, Yugoslavia, too. . . .

He was not in Moscow long, however, before he became uneasy about some of the things he observed. Instead of pure Socialism he found a reversion to free enterprise— the New Economic Policy (NEP)—which the Soviet Union had found necessary to work out of the ruins of war and revolution. Workers were overworked and underpaid. Women were paid less than men. Children were used in factories. Several families had to share a single room. Abandoned children begged on the streets, just as they had during Tsarist days.

"It is no simple matter to make over a whole society in eight years," he said loyally to Polga, as much to convince himself as her. "Yes, there are faults. But it is still better than it was under the Tsar. For most workers, anyhow. One day Comrade Stalin will make the Soviet Union an example to the world. Meanwhile, I must do what I can to help him free the workers in Yugoslavia!"

When it was time to return, Josip decided to leave Polga and Zarko with her parents, where they would be safe. His work would be more dangerous than ever; prison was inevitable. It had been so for Stalin; it would be so for him. He would send for his family after the revolution, and meanwhile see them whenever he could return to Russia.

Returning to Zagreb alone in April, 1927, he won easy election as full-time Secretary of the Metalworkers Union Regional Council. Serb police promptly arrested him. He demanded to know the charges. "Broz," one detective said wearily, "you have been in so much trouble we could arrest you at any time, and choose a dozen different charges!"

He was taken to jail at Ogulin to await trial as a Communist. Weeks passed and he still had not had his day in court. The police, he guessed, were not eager to rush the trial, fearing an uproar over the prosecution of so popular a trade union leader. Determined to force their hand, he declared a hunger strike. For five days he resolutely refused all food, growing so weak he could barely keep his feet. An unexpected plea to end his strike came from District Judge Stjepan Bakaric, who visited his cell personally.

Bakaric's compassion stemmed from the fact that his own son had strong Communist leanings, and was later to be made Prime Minister of the Croatian republic under Marshal Tito.

"*Ne,*" Josip shook his head stoically. "No. Either release me or try me. Starvation is better than rotting here!"

Bakaric promised him a swift trial, and had his wife send Josip a bowl of homemade soup. In October, 1927, Josip faced a state prosecutor who demanded his imprisonment for distributing subversive literature on the science of Marxism.

"What do the workers need scientific books for?" Judge Bakaric sighed to Josip in genuine bewilderment. "When their job is merely to chop things with an axe, or hit them with a hammer, why should they get interested in politics?"

He reluctantly sentenced Josip to seven months in jail, but gladly agreed to free him on bail pending an appeal by the Metalworkers Union lawyer. Josip returned to Zagreb to resume his union work. There was little doubt as to how the workers of Croatia felt about Josip Broz. He was promptly elected Secretary of both the Leatherworkers and Foodworkers Unions. Belgrade viewed him with rising anxiety.

The year 1928 saw widespread unrest throughout Yugoslavia because of unemployment, slashed wages, rising prices. Strikes and demonstrations were met by police brutal-

ity, provoking civil riots in city after city. It was a golden
opportunity for the illegal Yugoslav Communist Party, but
inter-Party feuds and poor leadership had reduced the ranks
to a bare three thousand underground members.

At a secret 8th Party Conference in Zagreb, on a snowy
night of February, 1928, Josip denounced the ineffective
Croat Party leaders and forced election of a militant new
Central Committee for the Zagreb area. He was made the
new Secretary. An impressed Comintern observer alerted
Moscow to keep an eye on Josip Broz as a promising leader
in the Balkans.

He organized fiery demonstrations in Zagreb for May
Day, 1928. Bloody clashes with the police led to mass arrests;
among the prisoners, of course, was Josip Broz.

Seething dissatisfaction with King Alexander's Serb-
dominated government was reflected in Parliament, where
the Croat Peasant Party denounced Serb brutality. On June
20 an enraged Serb deputy, provoked by Croat abuse, stood
up in Parliament, whipped out a pistol and shot Croatian
leader Stjepan Radic. Josip promptly organized three days
of protest and demonstration in the streets of Zagreb. An
urgent order flashed out from the highest authorities in Belgrade:

"Arrest Josip Broz—*and hold him!*"

But the police had to catch him first. Knowing that he
no longer dared operate openly, Josip began a new, completely illegal life under various aliases and disguises. An
actor friend of the Zagreb theatre showed him stage tricks
to alter his appearance. He ate and slept in the homes of
trusted comrades and unionists, never for longer than a day
or two, keeping constantly on the move. The police sought
him everywhere, and his margins of escape grew thinner.

The trail grew hotter on the tips of police informers.

One day, wearing dark glasses and overalls, he paid a
swift visit to his office at the Metalworkers Union. Two

policemen suddenly burst in. *"Stoy!"* one shouted. "Stop! Come on, we know he's here. Produce Broz!"

Josip, deep in conversation with a union official, lifted a scornful eyebrow. "Really? Where, policemen?" He waved his hand calmly around the office. "Don't you see he isn't here? Search if you like!"

The crestfallen policemen withdrew empty-handed.

On another occasion he was distributing arms to demonstrators from a loft. Police, tipped off by a spy, crashed through the front door. Josip sprang out the window onto an adjacent lower roof. Dropping through a skylight onto a butcher's display table loaded with pork, he made his getaway.

Late on the night of August 4, 1928, he was given a message begging help from comrades who had apparently fled to a room he maintained as a Party hideout. Hurrying there, he burst into the room only to have handcuffs snapped on both his wrists before he could draw the revolver he carried. He was too weary to struggle; he hadn't slept for forty-eight hours.

At police headquarters he was chained to a chair and kept there under strong lights for eight days and nights without sleep. Whenever his head began to nod, he was methodically beaten. "Not what you would call torture," he shrugged years later, "but my head and chest and arms were all black and blue." His jaws remained clamped under the persistent questions of the police. Where were the other Party officials? Where had he obtained the guns, hand grenades and Communist literature found in the flat he rented?

"Ne razumim," he replied stoically. "I don't understand. What brave fellows you are to beat a chained man!"

He spat blood as a chair smashed across his chest.

On the ninth day the disgusted police gave up. Josip was thrown into jail and kept there for three months.

Because by this time Josip Broz was a prominent controversial figure, his trial on November 6, 1928, commanded
national attention in the Yugoslav press. Cool, defiant, he
startled the court by freely admitting the charges against
him, but denying that they constituted any crime.

"I admit that I am a member of the outlawed Communist Party of Yugoslavia," he acknowledged. "I admit I
propagated the ideas of Communism; I described to the
workingmen all being done to them. I do not, however, recognize this bourgeois court, as I consider myself responsible
to the Communist Party alone!" It was bravado in the best
revolutionary tradition—using a capitalist courtroom, where
only conviction could be expected for Communists, as a
propaganda forum to arouse indignation at government
persecution.

Conducting his own defense, Josip charged the police
with planting arms and hand grenades in his flat in order
to frame the Party for the deaths of workers killed by police
during the June riots. (Years later, however, he laughed, "The
grenades were mine, all right.") He disclosed his brutal
interrogation by the police, and told of screams from the
cells of fellow prisoners. Accused of taking direction from
the Soviet Union, he replied defiantly, "Of course . . . we
are Moscow's organization!" It was a boast, not a confession.

Waiting for the verdict in his cell, Josip managed to
cut through five of six bars in the window with a file smuggled in to him in a loaf of bread. He deadened the noise by
putting moist bread around the file and bars. But before
he could file the sixth bar and escape, he was brought back
to the courtroom. Found guilty, he was sentenced to five
years in Lepoglava Prison, with five months added for his
conviction under appeal at Ogulin. Josip burst into a fiery
speech denouncing the ruling classes of Yugoslavia.

Silencing him angrily, the President of the court ordered
the session adjourned. Josip turned his back.

"What better proof could there be that this is a police state?" he cried out to the crowded courtroom. "Long live the Communist Party! Long live the world revolution!"

The courtroom fell into an uproar. Police fell upon the incorrigible firebrand and dragged him away to begin his imprisonment as a convicted enemy of the state.

Have Gun,
Will Travel

LEPOGLAVA was not the worst of prisons, having once been
a Pauline monastery nestled in a picturesque town on the
border of Josip's native Zagorje. But it was no bed of roses.
He had to bathe in a common tub of filthy ice water, wear
a uniform that was "a bundle of holes strung together," sleep
on a folding cot with two thin blankets in a freezing cell,
breakfast on a handful of bread and, worst of all, do without
books. He asked for a book on Greek philosophy.

The warden laughed. "What do you need that for, Broz?
Look around you—you'll see all the philosophy you want!"

The mechanical skill of the thirty-six-year-old revolutionist won him the job of caring for Lepoglava's small
power plant, on which the prison and town depended for
electricity. He soon had the run of the prison with test bulb
in one hand, screwdriver in the other. Permitted an assistant,
he chose spectacled, mustached Mosa Pijade, a brilliant
Jewish artist from Belgrade who was one of the Party's top
theoreticians. Josip helped Pijade organize a Communist
school within the prison. It was so effective two guards were
converted.

From time to time Josip would arrange to get to town under guard, ostensibly to make electrical repairs in the flat of Madame Fidlerica above her café, but actually to meet secretly there with comrades from Zagreb. They brought him Red tracts and requested works of literature, philosophy, sociology and political science. Downstairs in the café, meanwhile, Madame Fidlerica, a kindhearted, religious woman sympathetic to all unfortunates, would divert the guard with free drinks. When Josip was through with his "repairs" upstairs, the guard would escort him back to prison.

The smuggled books would be hidden in the floorboards of Pijade's cell, the prison "classroom." Pijade had no more eager pupil than Josip himself, who began delving into Shakespeare, the Greek philosophers, Thomas Paine and John Stuart Mill. He also reread Marx and Engels in the light of his more recent experiences, and discussed their ideas with Pijade as they puttered around the power plant.

"I made the prison my university," he recalled proudly thirty years later to US Supreme Court Justice William O. Douglas. Once he was asked whether his five-and-a-half-year imprisonment had embittered him toward King Alexander and his Serbian ministers. "Oh, no," he shrugged. "I was trying to overthrow their government. It was only natural that when they caught me, they should shut me up. I should have done the same in their place. In fact, I had every intension of doing the same when I *was* in their place!"

In 1929, alarmed by growing demonstrations against him, King Alexander, backed by the Army, made himself a dictator. The Yugoslav Parliament was suspended and Croats denied all voice in government. Suspected Communists were shot down on the streets in cold blood. Party leaders not already in jail like Josip and Pijade either were killed or fled abroad.

The Croat Peasant Party, forced underground as *Ustase*

(Rebels), was led by Dr. Ante Pavelic, a grim lawyer with a secret delight in terror and atrocities. Under his direction the Ustase began blowing up Serb trains, army barracks and police stations. They crowned their efforts by assassinating King Alexander in October, 1934.

Unwilling to let the Ustase seize revolutionary leadership from the Communist Party, Josip made an unsuccessful escape attempt in 1933. He was transferred to Yugoslavia's toughest prison at Maribor in Slovenia. Sleeping eight to a cell on straw floor mats, Josip sewed flour sacks for seven cents a month ("to give you a start on a decent life"), and fought the hordes of bedbugs and roaches that infested the walls. One day he was called to the warden's office.

"Broz, why haven't you asked for parole like the others?"

"The idea of release on parole is for the prisoner to correct himself, or at least show the desire to do so," Josip replied calmly. "But I do not want to renounce my political beliefs, so I do not ask to be released."

For this and other shows of defiance he was placed in solitary confinement. But he was anguished only by the grinding sounds of a clumsily handled locomotive switching freight cars in a nearby railroad siding. "All my mechanic's instincts rose in me," Josip later recalled wryly, "and I found myself wanting to yell, 'Mister, don't torture that engine!'"

As a final cruelty he was allowed to think he was being released on a cold November morning, only to be told at the last moment that he was being transferred to Ogulin Prison to serve three and a half more months on an earlier charge.

Finally, in March, 1934, he was freed under orders to stay out of all Yugoslav towns and remain in his home village of Kumrovec, where his father had died during his prison term. He was expected to report every day to the local police representative. These were absurd orders to give to a dedicated and ingenious conspirator. He stopped in Kumrovic only long enough to gather up from his brothers and sisters every photo, letter and document pertaining to Josip Broz, and burn them. Then he vanished.

Armed with forged documents of a dozen different names and identities, he reappeared in Zagreb with his hair dyed red, wearing a mustache and spectacles. Making contact with two comrades, he began rebuilding Zagreb's shattered Communist Party. Milovan Djilas, one of his two assistants, was an impetuous Montenegrin—intellectual, idealistic and uncompromising. The other, Alexander Rankovic, nicknamed Marko, was a tough peasant's son hardened by the class struggle. When his wife and mother were later murdered by Gestapo, he told Josip grimly, "Well, Socialism doesn't come cheap."

To receive instructions from Moscow and transmit reports, Josip frequently stole across the Yugoslav border, meeting Comintern agents in adjacent countries. His work for the Comintern sometimes took him to Paris, to assignation points in Germany and Switzerland and to Vienna, where the Yugoslav Communist Party now had its headquarters in exile.

Once he posed as a mountaineer crossing the Austrian Alps. His guide, hired to smuggle him past border guards, kept blackmailing him every few miles for more money. Josip finally booted him off and took his own chances, descending a dangerously deep ravine. He lost his grip and went crashing down the slope, ripping his clothes but making it safely to an Austrian farmhouse with no bones broken.

Sometimes he posed as a Czech businessman or German tourist, other times as an Austrian civil servant or Swiss bureaucrat. "No one," he once chuckled, "suspects a white, well-kept hand with a showy ring." His mastery of seven languages added credulity to his various disguises.

Once when a train was flagged down and checked on an informer's tip, he avoided suspicion by dandling a woman's baby on his smartly creased lap. The baby wet as

Josip handed his forged passport for inspection. Laughing, the policeman stamped the passport without examining it and handed it back. After all, Communists didn't look like that, or hold babies on their laps—or have such typical parental mishaps!

In September, 1934, Josip organized a Party conference in Slovenia under the noses of the police. Thirty delegates met at a beautiful estate in Medvode owned by the Bishop Rozman. Josip's host was the Bishop's black sheep half-brother, who had been banished here to keep him out of the way. For two days and nights the delighted Communists slept in the mansion and ate in a huge dining hall on white tableclothes set with fine crystal goblets and plates with the Bishop's coat-of-arms. "One day, Comrades," Tito assured them, "this will be a public museum. And if Bishop Rozman does not take care, he is likely to be one of the exhibits!"

It was at the Medvode Conference that Tito first met Edvard Kardelj, a quiet, mustached Slovene schoolmaster who had also been tortured by Serb police. They had held him out a sixth floor window by one leg, threatening to let him fall unless he turned informer. When he refused to be frightened, they had crushed his toes so that he was left with a permanent limp. He and Josip became close friends.

The Comintern was impressed with Josip's skill at holding secret Party conferences in Croatia and Slovenia and at evading capture during his travels for them. He was ordered to Moscow for special training in the Balkan Secretariat to prepare him for a major role in the future Yugoslav revolution. So in 1935, after a nine-year absence, he set out for the Soviet Union once more. He felt a surge of excitement as the train ground across the Polish frontier and he saw the red stars on the green caps of the border guards.

In all his agonized hours of torture, imprisonment and persecution, he had never felt alone or helpless. He saw himself as one of the rays of Socialism radiating around the world from the brilliant sun of the workers' homeland. Tuning in clandestinely whenever he could to midnight broadcasts from Radio Moscow, he had thrilled with pride as the Kremlin clock struck the hours to the stirring strains of the Communist "International" that called upon the "wretched of the earth" everywhere to arise against their oppressors.

And now, at last, he was back once more.

Becoming the Comintern representative for Yugoslavia under the new alias of "Comrade Walter," he was given a tiny office in the Comintern building near the Kremlin. His residence was a small room in the Hotel Lux reserved for foreign Communists, where he met the American Communist leader Earl Browder.

He made no attempt to visit Polga or their son Zarko, who was now twelve. During his imprisonment at Lepoglava, an impatient Polga wrote that she was divorcing him to marry a Russian. Josip took a stoical view of his loss. What else could have been expected of a pretty Soviet woman, married to a foreigner in jail in a foreign land, whom she might never see again?

He saw little of Moscow or its attractions, apart from an occasional ballet or opera at the Bolshoi Theater. Used to solitary years of reading and reflection in prison, "Comrade Walter" spent most of his spare time in his room studying economics, political philosophy and especially the military strategy of Frunze and Clausewitz. Someday he would be in command of revolutionary armies in Yugoslavia. The more he knew about military science, the more chance he would have of raising the Red Star over Belgrade.

He was delighted when lame Edvard Kardelj also showed up in Moscow, to study at the International Leninist School. The two friends were soon inseparable. In August, 1935, attending the 7th Comintern Congress together, they caught their first glimpse of Stalin. Fascinated, Josip saw a short Russian with large head, stiff mustache, sallow and pocked complexion, jagged yellow teeth clenched around a pipe. He was dressed in a peak cap, soft-collared tunic, clay-colored trousers and half-length top boots.

"Imagine," Josip whispered. "Stalin himself!"

"He looks bored," Kardelj observed.

"*Ne*, Edvard, not bored. Concerned! So would you be if you had to worry about revolution in fifty different countries!"

By 1936, Stalin was disgusted with the Yugoslav intellectuals whose constant quarrels had seriously weakened their Communist Party. A popular Comintern joke ran: "Two Yugoslavs—three factions!" With Fascism a growing threat in Europe, Moscow needed a strong man in the Balkans to serve as a red check to Hitler and Mussolini.

Georgi Dmitrov, then head of the Balkan section of the Comintern, urged Stalin to appoint Comrade Walter the new Organizing Secretary of the Yugoslav Party. Josip had proved himself a daring organizer; had spent almost as much time in prison as Stalin; was utterly loyal at a time when the Moscow trials, about to begin, had revealed a whole network of unsuspected treason at the highest levels of Bolshevik society. Stalin studied Josip's record and nodded assent.

Overwhelmed by the honor, Josip returned to Yugoslavia in April, 1936. To work now in the underground he had to change his identity as often as two and three times a day, although in Comintern communications he was always Comrade Walter.

Gradually, however, he developed a favorite new identity —"Tito." There were many theories as to what the name signified, the most popular alleging that the name in Serb-Croat means "You do." Grinning comrades insisted that Josip was always telling them, "You do this; you do that."

Amused, Tito refuted the speculation by explaining that the name was simply one that occurred to him after reading two Croat writers for whom Tito was a Christian name.

Tito, to refer to him now by his *nom de revolution*, devoted himself day and night to rebuilding the Yugoslav Communist Party underground. He put his life on the line every day as he traveled about the country developing a Red network. With typical audacity, and a peasant boy's delight in living in high style, he posed as a prosperous engineer.

Smartly dressed, he flashed a diamond ring on his carefully manicured fingers. He drove between cities in a Ford or traveled in first-class train or plane compartments. His waistline began to expand from an excess of rich pastries, goulash and coffee with whipped cream. But his deception was audaciously successful. Who would look for a "dirty Red" in so distinguished a bourgeois gentleman? Instead of clapping him into jail, police saluted him deferentially.

"Riches of the mind mean nothing in a corrupt society," Tito scoffed. "What counts is riches on your back!"

Aided by Kardelj, Tito built the Yugoslav Communist Party to a strength of twelve thousand in three years. Most of their recruits were hand-picked intellectuals and radicals prepared to lay down their lives for the Party—and Joseph Stalin.

When the Spanish Civil War broke out on July 17, 1936, Tito received special orders from Dmitrov to recruit as many Balkan volunteers as possible to fight with the Loyalists against the Fascist Franco. The Comintern knew that Hitler and Mussolini planned to use Spain as a testing ground to see how far the democracies would allow Fascism to go. Stalin did not dare intervene openly, but he considered it imperative that an International Brigade be raised to fight in Madrid for the Spanish republic. If Spain fell to Fascism, Hitler might feel encouraged to turn his armies eastward to

attack Moscow, confident that the Western powers would
make no move to stop him. Tito understood the peril to the
Mecca of the world's workers, and responded swiftly.

He organized an underground railroad by which recruits for Spain were shipped to Barcelona through officially
neutral Zurich and Marseilles. Anxious to fight Fascism himself, he begged Dmitrov for permission to go to Spain. His
request was turned down. Comrade Walter was too valuable
as a recruiting agent. Singlehandedly, he had raised two
complete battalions of volunteers, the largest Balkan con-
tingent in the International Brigade. Half of the Yugoslav
volunteers were killed in action. A third were wounded.

Tito himself narowly escaped death in his travels to
raise and smuggle the Spanish-bound volunteers. Once, returning through France, he was deep in fatigued sleep when
a German frontier guard shook him awake crossly, asking
his name. Too groggy to remember the name on the passport
he was carrying, he pretended not to understand German,
stalling for time until he could fish out the passport and steal
a surreptitious glance at it to find out who he was.

Once he made the mistake of using a Canadian passport
in Copenhagen. The policeman checking it began a friendly
conversation in English. Tito, whose English was the poorest of the languages he had mastered, stammered a few
clumsily phrased replies. He waited tensely for a clap on his
shoulder—"detained for questioning." But the Danish policeman only smiled dryly and winked. Apparently a Left-wing
sympathizer, he passed on whispering, "Next time, Comrade,
learn better English before using a Canadian passport!"

Tito had his moments of doubt about the wisdom of his
choice to live as a hard-core Communist. Did he risk his
life out of a profound devotion to Socialism, he wondered,
or was he simply a born troublemaker and adventurer? In a
philosophical, self-searching mood, he impulsively returned
one day in 1937, in disguise, to his origins—the sleepy

little village of Kumrovec. What had tempted him from this sylvan backwater to the arena of world politics?

Wandering in the hilly meadows where he had once herded the family cows, he watched again the worn, ragged village peasants and their half-starved children going about their centuries-old toil in mud and squalor. He sat there reflecting as twilight fell. When he returned to Zagreb he felt reassured about the motives that drove him. Someday, he vowed, all the Kumrovecs of Yugoslavia would be lifted out of their backward misery by a Communist regime that would bring them a new life through industry and electrification.

That summer he received a sudden order to return to Moscow at the height of the sensational treason trials that had followed Stalin's decision to purge the Party. Leading Soviet bureaucrats and generals were being publicly denounced, forced to confess crimes against the state, then herded off for swift execution. Djilas was apprehensive.

"Perhaps you're on the list," he warned.

"*Me?*" Tito laughed. "*Nemoguche!* Impossible. Everyone knows I am absolutely loyal to Comrade Stalin."

But he was stunned, upon arriving in Moscow, to find that the Yugoslav representatives at the Comintern had been denounced and arrested. "It was obvious that the Comintern was not keeping to its democratic principles," he wrote later. "My whole being rebelled against what I saw in Moscow."

He found administrative chaos. Thousands of Red officials were swept away by mass midnight arrests. Russians dreaded to ask questions about vanished relatives or friends, let alone protest any injustice. Upset, Tito still stubbornly refused to let these unpleasant discoveries shake his devotion to Stalin and world Communism.

"It was my revolutionary duty at the time," he lamely apologized years later, "not to criticize or help alien propa-

ganda against that country, for at that time it was the only
country where a revolution had been carried out and where
Socialism had to be built." If he had acknowledged disillusionment, he could not have remained a Communist.

Dmitrov had startling news for him. The Comintern
had decided that he, Comrade Walter, should take over the
whole Yugoslav Party temporarily as its new Secretary General.

Tito, now forty-five, a veteran of twenty-seven years in
the labor movement, blinked incredulously. Even a temporary appointment of such magnitude was a tremendous
honor.

"What do you intend to do first?" Dmitrov asked.

"Move Party headquarters to Zagreb," Tito replied without hesitation. He had long felt it a mistake for the Party
to operate legally from the distance of Vienna. Yugoslav
workers needed Party leaders among them in the underground, encouraging them, giving them on-the-spot direction, coordinating their efforts, sharing their hardships and
risks, planning guerrilla attacks on the police who oppressed
them. During King Alexander's dictatorship between 1929
and 1935 over thirty-five thousand political prisoners had
been thrown in jail and tortured. Prince Paul now ruled in
the name of his boy cousin, King Peter. Tito told Dmitrov
his second objective:

"I'm going to end factional disputes. We need a united
Party leadership that will permit us to use all our energies
fighting the government—not each other!"

"Better Grave Than Slave!"

RETURNING to Zagreb, Tito summoned the comrades he
trusted to serve as his lieutenants—Edvard Kardelj, Milovan
Djilas, Marko Rankovic. Joining them was a member of the
old Central Committee who had survived Stalin's purge—
Sretan "Black" Zujovic, a tall, dark Serb revolutionist who
had fought in the French Foreign Legion. Kardelj and
Djilas were veterans of the Spanish Civil War; along with
the others who had fought Franco, they were known as "the
Spaniards."

To his followers, the forty-five-year-old Yugoslav leader
was known affectionately as "the Old Man." They were
utterly devoted to him, inspired by his leadership, sharing
his confidence in the ultimate triumph of their struggle to
bring Socialism to Yugoslavia. They also accepted his un-
questioning faith in Joseph Stalin and the Soviet Union.

Tito was convinced that international Fascism, with the
tacit consent of the Western democracies, was preparing to
attack Moscow. Following Comintern instructions, he agi-
tated for a Yugoslav defense alliance with the Soviet Union

47

against Nazi Germany and Fascist Italy. But in August, 1939, Stalin suddenly signed a Non-Aggression Pact of friendship with the monster of monsters, Adolph Hitler.

Tito and his followers were thunderstruck. He stared unbelievingly at instructions from Moscow to stop agitating against Fascism, and to concentrate Party attacks on the "decadent imperialist nations"—the United States, Britain and France—"who had schemed to drive Germany and the Soviet Union into war to destroy them both, so that the Western capitalists could then take over all of Europe."

Edvard Kardelj was deeply skeptical. "I can accept the fact that Stalin is buying time to prepare Soviet defenses against a German invasion," he told Tito. "But if Hitler was a Fascist beast yesterday, why isn't he still a Fascist beast *today*? How can we suddenly stop denouncing him or the Fascism we fight as the enemy of workers everywhere?"

"We must maintain Communist discipline," Tito insisted. "That means accepting the pact. Moscow knows best. We must explain to comrades that the Berlin-Moscow Pact is a necessary tactic for Stalin. He's foiled the plan of the West to lure Hitler into destroying the Soviet fatherland because they're afraid of its example to their own workers!"

"You sound," Milovan Djilas said dryly, "very much like a man desperately trying to convince himself!"

Tito made several trips to Moscow to talk to Dmitrov, who warned him that the Kremlin still distrusted the Yugoslav Communist movement as too "undisciplined." One day Tito had lunch at the Lux with Veljko Vlahovic, a Montenegrin Party member who had lost a leg in Spain and was now the Yugoslav representative to the Comintern.

"Do you notice," he whispered to Tito, "that none of the other Comintern members care to sit at our table?"

"It doesn't matter," Comrade Walter shrugged. "One

day they'll be grabbing chairs from each other to sit with us!"

He refused to let his faith in Stalin be shaken, even though he became increasingly troubled by the Soviet invasion of Finland and the partition of Poland with Hitler.

When the invasion of Poland by Hitler led Britain and France to declare war on Germany, Tito followed the Comintern lead in denouncing the conflict as an imperialist war like World War I, in which all workers could have no possible interest except to keep out of it. He organized several peace demonstrations by Yugoslav workers, and planned a campaign to sabotage the Royal Army in case the government tried to take the nation into the war on the Allied side.

"We are not interested in the bourgeois ideal of a fatherland to be defended," he told his Central Committee, "but of a world revolution to be won."

At each new turn and twist of the Moscow line, a new group of Party comrades would balk at swallowing it. Tito would reason with them along practical lines. There could be no dissent or doubt once the Comintern had taken a position. Only Party discipline mattered. But the ranks of the YCP grew progressively thinner. Those who remained loyal to the Kremlin were the most seasoned revolutionaries— tough, unshakable, prepared to follow wherever the Kremlin led.

"We've paid heavily for the Stalin-Hitler pact," Djilas said, discouraged. "Our membership is way down."

"Perhaps it's for the best," Tito cheered him. "Remember that Lenin said revolutions are made by a small, tight band of professional revolutionists—not by a large, democratically led political party!"

Traveling through Yugoslavia constantly in his repertory of disguises, often going days and nights without sleep, he found time to fall in love and marry again. Herta, a pretty young Slovene Communist, bore him a son, Alexander, whom Tito nicknamed Misko. But his family saw little of him as the rush of world events brought fresh dangers to the Balkans. Like all Yugoslavs, Tito grew increasingly uneasy as the Hitler war machine overran northern Europe, then swept south, making satellites of Hungary, Rumania and Bulgaria. The ring around Yugoslavia grew tighter with the Italian grab of Albania and invasion of Greece.

Under the regency of Prince Paul, Yugoslavia had been restored to constitutional government. Home rule had been granted to the Croats, although Serb-Croat hostility was as bitter as ever. The war had added fuel to the flames.

The Serbs hated the Germans, whom they had fought in World War I, and admired the British, their former ally. The Croats, who had been forced to fight Serbs on the Hapsburg side, were either pro-German or neutral. Both sides pressed the government to support the side they favored.

Prince Paul and his advisers, worried about a German invasion of Yugoslavia, tried to appease Hitler. But in the spring of 1941, Hitler had already decided to attack the Soviet Union. Before he could launch Operation Barbarossa, he needed to protect his rear from possible landings by the Allies on the Adriatic coast of Yugoslavia, his last vulnerable spot in the "soft underbelly" of the Balkans.

In March, 1941, Prince Paul and his advisers were summoned by Hitler and flatly ordered to sign a Tripartite Pact aligning Yugoslavia with the Axis powers. They signed.

Serbia exploded in wild indignation. A group of Serb officers in the Yugoslav Air Force staged a coup d'etat in Belgrade and overthrew the government. A new neutralist regime was set up under young Prince Peter as the new King, and General Dusan Simovic as Prime Minister.

"The Yugoslav nation has found its soul!" enthusiastically declared England's Prime Minister Winston Churchill.

Hitler refused to believe the news at first. Assured it was true, he flew into a towering rage and screamed orders for the immediate destruction of Yugoslavia.

"The beginning of Operation Barbarossa," he snapped at his generals, "will be postponed for four weeks." The delay was actually six weeks—a fatal turn of events for Hitler's plan of world conquest. It trapped the invading Nazi forces in the sub-zero winter of Russia three to four weeks short of the time they needed to achieve a lightning total victory, giving Stalin time to recover and mount a counterattack.

But in March, 1941, Hitler assured Ribbentrop he would make short work of Yugoslavia, which would then he sliced up among Italy, Hungary and Rumania, with Croatia set aside as a small puppet state. Stalin, who still did not suspect that Operation Barbarossa was imminent, nevertheless did not want to see the Balkans fall under Hitler's control. So on April 5 in Moscow he signed a "Friendship and Non-Aggression Pact" with the new government of King Peter. He hoped that this gesture of guarded support would make Hitler hesitate to attack Belgrade.

But the very next morning 51 mechanized Axis divisions —24 German, 22 Italian, 5 Hungarian—thundered across the borders of Yugoslavia. Two hours later 1,500 German bombers rained destruction down upon the helpless city of Belgrade. During three days and nights of "Operation Punishment"—Hitler's own name for it—20,000 Belgrade civilians were killed and thousands more wounded.

The city's water system was destroyed so that incendiary fires could not be put out; then homes, hospitals, churches, schools and libraries were dive-bombed and Stukas flew at rooftop level to reduce the city to charred ruins. Even the zoo was bombed, releasing badly burned polar bears and other animals to roam through the smoking rubble.

On April 13 German and Hungarian troops took what was left of the capital, and four days later the 28 divisions of the Yugoslav Army surrendered at Sarajevo. King Peter and Prime Minister Simovic escaped by plane to Greece, then flew on to London to set up a government in exile.

Jubilant, Hitler set up a military government in Belgrade, created the "Independent State of Croatia," and divided the rest of Yugoslavia among German, Italian, Hungarian and Bulgarian occupation troops. A Serb puppet named Nedic was set up to head Serbia, and secretly encouraged to massacre Moslems and Croats in his region. As Fascist dictator of Croatia, Hitler installed in Zagreb the Ustase leader, Dr. Ante Pavelic, who had had King Alexander murdered.

Hitler was using the classic "divide-and-rule" ploy of conquerors to keep Yugoslavs at each others' throats, to keep them from uniting against the invaders.

Pavelic promptly announced his intention to "purify" Croatia of gypsies, Serbs and Jews: "The Serbs are alien elements on Croat territory. . . . They are rebels and as rebels they must be treated." His Minister of Education and Religion was even more explicit on June 6th at a banquet.

"We shall kill some of the Serbs," he promised, "we shall expel others, and the remainder will be forced to embrace the Roman Catholic faith." For all minorities in Croatia, he announced grimly, "We have three million bullets."

The Archbishop of Zagreb and Metropolitan of Croatia, Monsignor Aloysius Stepinac, accepted appointment as Archvicar of Pavelic's army, and called upon the clergy to support the new dictatorship. "These are events," he wrote, "which fulfill the long dreamed of and desired ideal of our people. . . . Respond readily to my call to join the noble task of working for the safety and well-being of the Independent State of Croatia."

Bands of fanatical Ustase shock troops began roaming the countryside with knives, grenades and machine guns, massacring thousand of Serbs, slaughtering Jews, strangling suspected Communists. Orthodox Serbian churches were set afire with their screaming congregations inside; worshippers who sought to flee the flames were shot as they ran out.

Many Serbs in Croatia fled to the hills of central Serbia to join the guerrilla ranks of the Chetniks, headed by Draza Mihailovic, a colonel of the Yugoslav Army. He had been left behind by King Peter and Simovic to organize a resistance movement against the Germans. A tall, majestic-looking Serb with a flowing beard and high sheepskin hat, Mihailovic was made a general by the London government in exile, which also appointed him its Minister of War and promised that England would smuggle in arms and supplies to support Chetnik operations against the enemy.

But Mihailovic was cautious about making guerrilla attacks that might provoke savage reprisals by the Germans. A conservative monarchist, he was more worried about the possibility of revolution in Yugoslavia than about its Fascist occupation. Many of his officers pressed him to collaborate with Nedic's puppet Serb government.

As for Tito, the events of April, 1941, caught him by surprise. He looked to Moscow for a Party line to take toward the bewildering, rapid sequence of events that had followed Prince Paul's abortive Tripartite Pact with Hitler. But Stalin himself was confused, not sure of Hitler's real intentions toward Russia or of the safest way to play power politics in the Balkans. Attempting to fathom Kremlin policy, Tito called for neutrality toward all developments in the "imperialist war," even though it had now spilled over into his native land.

There could be no possibility, he felt, of supporting the Simovic government in exile, which had now taken a firm stand on the side of England against the Axis. In fact, Tito even urged cooperation with the Ustase to root out all traces of the old Serb monarchy, infiltrate Pavelic's Croat administration to subvert it, and steal Ustase arms to store in a secret Communist arsenal for their own revolution.

But Black Zujovic was uneasy. "How can we just stand aside," he protested, "while the Germans and Italians occupy our country? The Yugoslav people won't endure it!"

"It's only temporary," Tito assured him. "Sooner or later the Soviet Union will enter the war—when Comrade Stalin feels the time is ripe. *Then* we fight, Comrades. Not for the King or British imperialism, but in support of the Soviet Union, for a Red Yugoslavia and a Red world!"

Milovan Djilas looked thoughful, but said nothing.

It was a shortsighted policy, the inevitable consequence of Tito's blind faith in Stalin. But it was no more shortsighted than Stalin's own disbelief of British Intelligence warnings that Hitler was preparing to attack him.

Ironically, it kept Tito from beginning guerrilla warfare against the Nazis in Yugoslavia between April 6 and June 22, 1941. Lost were over ten weeks of vital time when a fierce Partisan uprising might have forced Hitler to delay his attack on the Soviet Union even longer than the six weeks that it cost him to run up the swastika over Yugoslavia.

But on June 22, when the German blitzkrieg rolled across the Soviet border, Tito at once called upon the workers and peasants of Yugoslavia for a guerrilla war against the invaders. "The hour has struck to take arms for your freedom against Fascist aggression," he declared in a proclamation printed on secret presses and carried to all parts of the nation. "Do your part in the fight for freedom under the leadership of the Communist Party of Yugoslavia. The war of the Soviet Union is your war, because the Soviet Union is fighting against your enemies, under whose yoke your neck is bent." And he gave Yugoslavs a fiery war cry:

"Better grave than slave!"

Once the die was cast, there was to be no more courageous anti-Fascist fighter in Yugoslavia than Josip Broz Tito.

With characteristic daring, he did not take to the hills like Mihailovic, but moved from Zagreb to the center of the German occupation—Belgrade. He set up his headquarters under the noses of the Nazis, in a fashionable villa owned by a wealthy newspaper owner and sympathizer only a few hundred yards away from the official residence of the German Commander-in-Chief.

A removable washbasin concealed a passageway to a roof hiding place where he kept a cache of hand grenades and revolvers. When it was necessary for him to leave the villa, he carried a revolver and two grenades to help him fight out of any tight spots. The Germans knew him as a stout, affluent engineer called Slavko Babic—a typically flashy bourgeois type who reminded them of Hermann Goering.

One day a secret rendezvous with Kardelj took Tito past the charred Belgrade National Library. The book-loving revolutionist stared in anguish at the ruined rare books and medieval manuscripts, priceless documents of Yugoslav history, strewn in the rubble of the library basement. A helmeted German soldier passed by, a submachine gun slung across his chest. "Never in my life," Tito later related fiercely, "had I looked with so much hatred at anyone as I looked at this German soldier!"

A magnificent organizer, he soon had spies in the agency that transmitted official German confidential bulletins. Aware of the movements of Nazi commanders in and around Belgrade even before they knew themselves, he skillfully coordinated the attacks of Communist guerrilla units, now known as Partisans. German troops walked into traps or were blown to bits in transit. Sabotage squads cut phone lines, attacked Nazis in dark streets and stole their weapons, set German vehicles afire by dropping delayed incendiaries in gas tanks. Dismayed Nazi commanders ordered swift reprisals.

Wall posters went up all over Serbia: FOR EVERY GER-MAN WHO IS FOUND KILLED, ONE HUNDRED SERBS WILL BE SHOT.

Nazi squad cars circled Belgrade, directed by Nedic's traitor police to point out suspected Partisan saboteurs. Soldiers would open fire with light machine guns.

The Partisans dynamited a train near Kragujevac, killing 50 German troops and injuring 100. The enraged district commander promptly machine-gunned 9,000 Yugoslav civilians. Teachers were compelled to march their pupils from classrooms to the firing range, where they were mowed down in rows.

Mihailovic was outraged—but not at the Nazis. That madman Tito! Was it worth 9,000 Yugoslav lives for the satisfaction of killing and wounding 150 Nazis? To Tito that was the reasoning of a toothless lion. The Nazis must learn that they could not move safely through Yugoslavia. Besides, the massacre of 9,000 innocent Yugoslavs would enrage 90,-000 more into risking their lives to kill Nazis.

Tito sent Milovan Djilas to lead the Partisan forces in Montenegro. Edvard Kardelj became the leader of the guerrillas in Slovenia. Marko Rankovic and Black Zujovic carried out operations in the Serbian mountains. Alerted by the intelligence bulletins from "Slavko Babic" in Belgrade, they cut phone and power lines, blew up bridges and airfield hangars, smashed newspapers peddling the Nazi line, and created confusion by sabotaging files in German-held towns.

In Kraljevo a Serb peasant waited behind a tree with an axe until a Nazi motorcyclist approached on the road; a swing of the axe and the Kraljevo Partisans got their first submachine gun. In Kragujevac a Partisan squad obtained their first six army rifles by holding up a police post with unloaded sports rifles. Soon police stations all over Serbia were being held up and looted of arms.

The Nazis fought back furiously with mass executions

of thousands of bewildered Yugoslav peasants. Bodies were left dangling on trees and lamp posts as warnings. On July 27, 1941, Rankovic was captured in Belgrade and held for questioning at Gestapo headquarters, although the Germans did not suspect his identity as a Partisan leader.

Tito went to his rescue swiftly. Partisans masquerading as Gestapo detectives won entry into the headquarters cell section and snatched Rankovic free with false orders before the Germans realized they had been tricked.

The difference between the resistance movements of Tito and Mihailovic became increasingly clear to the Yugoslav people, not only in vigor but in ultimate aims. The Chetnik leader intended to restore the monarchy and the old way of life that went with it. Tito was frankly fighting for a Communist Yugoslavia, even though he called the Partisan struggle a "people's war," and welcomed all anti-Fascists.

In August, 1941, with the Nazis turning Belgrade upside down to find him, he finally left to take command in the field of a Partisan army of 12,000 Communists, 15,000 teen-age members of the Young Communist League and 200,000 sympathizers. Astonishingly, one in four of his volunteer guerrillas was a woman. "We love our country as much as the men," one girl Partisan explained. "Besides, we're far safer roughing it with the Partisans than we would be if we stayed behind under those horrible Nazis and their Ustase pigs!"

Feud in the Mountains

A STERN disciplinarian, Tito kept his followers not only from stealing food from peasants and from drinking, but also from making even mildly romantic approaches to women Partisans. Understandably, some male guerrillas grumbled that a few harmless kisses here and there might work wonders for their morale. But Tito wanted no distractions in the fight for freedom.

Both male and female Partisans had to take the oath he had written: "We, the people's Partisans of Yugoslavia, have taken up arms to wage a relentless struggle against the bloodthirsty enemies who have enslaved our country and are exterminating our peoples. In the name of liberty and justice for our people, we swear that we shall be disciplined, persevering and fearless. That we shall spare neither blood nor life in fighting the Fascist invaders and all traitors to the people until they are completely annihilated."

Most Partisan units began with a drastic shortage of weapons, sometimes only shotguns and axes. Tito's own unit dug up the tiny cache of rifles, pistols and hand grenades he had buried some twenty years earlier near the village of Veliko Trojstvo, when he had been arrested on a priest's accusation. Most Partisan arms, however, came from daring raids on Axis outposts—particularly on Italian garrisons.

Petrol or ammunition dumps that could not be captured were blown up. Large areas of the countryside, villages and hamlets, began falling under Partisan control. Proudly radioing reports of his progress to Moscow, Tito pleaded for arms drops by Soviet planes. Kremlin replies were limited to warm praise and encouragement for Partisan exploits.

New recruits flowed steadily into Tito's army as a result of atrocities committed by the Ustase against the Serbs, and Nazi reprisals against peasants for Partisan raids. The struggle grew bloodier and more horrifying, with terrible vengeance taken by both sides.

In Macra the Germans slaughtered men, women and children, then covered their bodies with flour to dispose of them to hungry pigs. At Cajetina, German tanks wounded sixty Partisans, then deliberately ran over them as they tried to crawl away. At Kosjeric, Chetnik police mistreated and killed seventeen Partisans, some of them girls, then threw them in a fire. Ustase burned the town of Rogatica; nailed horseshoes on an Orthodox priest's hands and knees, saddled and rode him through town. Then they slaughtered all Moslems "taller than a rifle." It was typical of the savage bitterness Catholic Croats felt toward Orthodox Serbs and Moslems.

Tito felt strongly that the Germans and their Yugoslav collaborators were to be fought against as one and the same. "In their struggle against the invaders," he declared in a Party speech, "the Serbian people will have to wage a no less determined struggle against the traitors."

Of all his enemies, he considered the Italians the most humane. "They have left the schools alone and even want to build a new university for the Slovenes," he reported to the Comintern in May, 1941. "The Italians are also behaving decently in Dalmatia and in Montenegro. The soldiers quickly make friends . . . saying they have had enough of the war."

Despite Nazi, Ustase and Chetnik atrocities, he refused to allow Partisan retaliation. "Upon pain of death," he ordered on November 8, 1941, "it is forbidden to react to these crimes by taking similar countermeasures." It was brave to blow up a troop train; cowardly to inflict personal violence upon a helpless prisoner. Partisan honor must not be compromised by imitating contemptible behavior.

Impressed by Tito's brand of warfare, some Chetnik units attacked German outposts without authority from Mihailovic. These raids, added to Partisan attacks, compelled the Germans to pull back from a greater part of Serbia in the autumn of 1941. Some provinces fell under Partisan control, others under the Chetniks. By mid-September Tito decided to propose to Mihailovic that they join forces.

Accompanied by fifteen young Partisans, he rode into a Chetnik village to meet the bearded Serb general. Face to face for the first time, the revolutionist and the royalist stared at each other in equal fascination. Tito found himself agreeably impressed by Mihailovic's mild, pleasant manner. The Chetnik, in turn, was surprised that the Communist looked so typically Yugoslavian; he had been almost convinced that Tito was actually a native of Russia.

Over a Serbian village meal Tito outlined his plan for a combined attack to drive the Germans out of Serbia. Mihailovic listened dubiously. He suspected the shrewd Communist leader of a scheme to absorb the Chetniks into the Partisan army. He shook his head.

"Your plans are too reckless. Even if we combine our forces, we cannot match the German strength. We would be wiped out, and the Germans would take a terrible revenge on the people. No, let us each pursue our own strategy."

The meeting ended amicably, but Tito left convinced that the King's general was much too timid to take any essential risks against the Germans; certainly he was no ally for Partisan forces to depend upon.

At his headquarters in the mountain village of Stolice, he called a conference of all his Partisan commanders in other parts of the country. From now on, he told them, each Partisan force will run its own guerrilla war. Pitched battles were to be avoided; German units were to be knocked out by hit-and-run attacks. Each liberated area would be governed as a Russian-style Soviet under a "National Liberation Council." Captured traitors and collaborators would be tried and punished by local "people's courts."

Vigorous application of these tactics began bringing district after district under Partisan control. Some Chetnik leaders, impressed by Tito's militancy and disgusted with Milhailovic's inaction, defected with their units to the Partisans. Mihailovic grew alarmed at these developments.

Propaganda broadcasts by the Simovic government-in-exile in London were giving the world the impression that only Mihailovic was fighting a war of resistance in the mountains of Yugoslavia. Tito and the Partisans were almost unknown in the West, whose leaders were promising all-out aid to "the heroic Chetniks and their valiant leader."

Mihailovic decided to fight—but not the Germans. If his Chetniks wiped out the Partisans, they would be saving Yugoslavia from Communism, if not Fascism. The Germans, he was sure, would even help them. As for the Germans, their fate would automatically be settled by the outcome of the war in Russia. So why waste valuable Serb lives in futile attempts to drive them out of Yugoslavia now?

When he was forced to defend this decision five years later at a trial for his life, Mihailovic declared pathetically, "I wanted nothing for myself. . . . I had against me a competitive organization—the Yugoslav Communist Party—

which seeks its own ends without compromise. I found my-self in a whirl of events and intrigues. . . . The whirlwind, the whirlwind of the world, carried me and my work away."

In November, 1941, he unleashed his Chetnik forces in a full-scale attack against Partisan headquarters at Uzice. It failed, but other clashes followed. Soon, to the great delight of the Germans, the rival guerrilla forces of Yugoslavia were fighting a bitter civil war. Pressed on one side by Mihailovic, on the other by what became known as the First Enemy Offensive of November–December, 1941, Tito withdrew his forces to the mountains of east Bosnia.

To cover their retreat and observe the direction of the pursuing German thrust, he stayed behind with a small squad of guerrillas. A flying column of Nazi troops overran his position. Narrowly escaping capture, Tito journeyed twenty wintry miles to rejoin his forces, every mile on foot and under intense enemy fire. When he turned up at Par-tisan headquarters, where he had been given up for dead, he was embraced joyfully by Djilas and Kardelj.

Too exhausted to speak, he simply put down his sub-machine gun and slumped into a chair. Kardelj filled him in rapidly on the military situation. Only after he had worked out dispositions for the 80,000 Partisans fighting under his command did he wearily ask if he might have some water.

On December 21, 1941, Stalin's birthday, Tito formed the First Proletarian Brigade—his first transformation of guerrilla bands into a formal army unit. These shock troops had Spanish veteran Koca Popovic for their leader, and wore fur caps with red stars embossed with a hammer and sickle.

With Serbia back in their hands, the Germans punished the peasants who had fed and sheltered the Partisans. Over 9,000 were shot—300 for each German who had been killed. They also burned 17 villages to the ground.

"It was Tito who caused this," Mihailovic charged bitterly. "I warned him!" He began to collaborate with the Germans, secretly at first, openly later, in hunting down Partisan units. As his reward, his forces were armed and supplied by the Germans, who left the Chetniks alone. One of Mihailovic's huge bodyguards kept a large wooden chest strapped to his back at all times, ready to flee if the Partisans suddenly attacked. It contained Mihailovic's treasury.

Tito's men, half-starved and freezing in the Bosnian winter, their ranks full of wounded, escaped the German offensive only to have to fight their way through the Italians. Black Zujovic was shot in the stomach, but not fatally.

Tito kept Partisan morale high by fighting in the forefront of his men, exhorting them to remember that Russia's Red Army, too, had suffered before achieving victory. Their spirits were also raised by the knowledge that now Yugoslavs everywhere were beginning to support them, turning against Mihailovic as a traitor to the Resistance. Tito felt proud that Serbs, Croats, Slovenes, Bosnians, Montenegrins and Dalmatians had put aside their ancient feuds for the first time in history to fight under him voluntarily as Yugoslav comrades in arms, united by common hatred of the enemy.

Some of the fiercest fighters in Tito's ranks were the Serbs who had lost loved ones to the torture, rape and murder of Pavelic's brutal Ustase. Hundreds of Serb women and children had been hurled alive off cliffs. Some Ustase collected parts of their victims' bodies as trophies to display proudly in Zagreb cafés as they boasted of their murders. One Ustase would display peasants' eyes he carried, laughing, "My eyes are not too good, so I took these as spares. No sense in burying fine eyes like these!"

Even their Nazi overlords were sickened by the senseless cruelties of the Ustase. Monsignor Stepinac, who had begun by blessing Pavelic's "crusade," ended by urging him to halt his barbaric atrocities. On the other hand, Archbishop

Saric of Sarajevo praised Pavelic extravagantly for winning so many "converts" for Rome.

"Pavelic is an idiot," Tito told a British observer later. "For every Serb, Croat or Bosnian his cuthroats massacre or torture, a dozen others join us to kill Ustase. If Hitler meant to frighten our people into submission with Pavelic and his beasts, he doesn't know Yugoslavs!"

As Tito's numbers grew in Bosnia, spearheaded by the First Proletarian Brigade, the Germans and Ustase launched the Second Enemy Offensive (January–February, 1942). Tito found his forces split by Nazi ski troops spearing through the deep snow from the north while Italians encircled them from the south. But he managed to slip through the noose, uniting his forces and leading them over the high mountain passes of the Jahorina at temperatures of twenty below. Over 150 Partisan men and women suffered so severely from frostbite that their limbs had to be amputated without anesthetics, using woodsaws boiled in hot water.

Tito set up a new headquarters at the tiny Bosnian village of Foca, above the gorge of the Drina. Foca had already changed hands several times. One storekeeper was found to have four different flags under his counter—German, Italian, Ustase and Partisan. When he heard fighting going on around town, he would listen carefully, then display the flag of the victor. "Poor man," Tito later commented wryly. "When the Partisans withdrew, he was shot by the Italians because they found our flag under the counter."

A steady influx of recruits swelled Partisan ranks at Foca until Tito had five battalions. Short of arms, food, clothes and medical supplies, they were fully equipped with *esprit de corps*. They were proud to be Partisans, careful to make a good impression on the peasants they moved among.

"Here we are among our own people," Tito reminded

them. "We must depend upon them for support, concealment, information, food and recruits. They must see for
themselves that we Partisans are not the monsters the enemy
tries to paint us, but decent neighbors who care about and
respect them. We cannot, therefore, tolerate any violation
of discipline."

One day a Partisan was brought before him charged
with an act of sabotage. The accused man, recovering from
typhus, had been tempted by the sight of a peasant sowing
barley in a plowed field. When the peasant had passed by,
he had dug the grains out of a furrow with his fingers and
devoured them one by one. The peasant had caught him
at it.

"You know the penalty for stealing food from our own
people," Tito said coldly. "What is your defense?"

"I was starved, Comrade," the man whispered.

Tito's eyes blurred. But in a low voice he ordered the
offender shot. He tied the bandage around the doomed
Partisan's eyes with his own hands. "Forgive me, Comrade.
But I can make no exceptions. If for you, then for another.
Once I condone crimes against our people, they would soon
think us no better than Nazis, Chetniks or Ustase. Then we
would lose their support in our fight to free the country."

Then a Partisan rifle squad carried out the execution.
The peasant who had brought the charges watched, awed
and impressed. Tito knew his words and action would spread
through the mountains, reassuring peasants, cautioning Partisans.

Elsewhere in Yugoslavia, beyond Tito's immediate control, some Partisan units avoided his tight discipline. Montenegrin guerrillas were fierce zealots who preferred to wipe
out any and all political opponents ruthlessly. They provoked
Chetnik attacks by boldly proclaiming Montenegro to be a
province of the Soviet Union. Tito was exasperated by such

clumsy tactics. Didn't the fools realize that 99 percent of his
recruits now were not radicals but simple peasants—most
of them "politically very backward"?

It was vitally important not to lose the kind of popular
support he found at the village of Previle on January 24,
1942. The peasants welcomed the Partisans with open joy.

"*Hvala*," an old lady told Tito gratefully. "Thank you.
If it wasn't for you people, the Germans would have burned
the whole Jahorina region to the ground." When her husband growled something at her, she snapped back, "You
can't shout at me, now, *gospodin* [Mister]—the Partisans are
here!"

Struggling against the Second Enemy Offensive, Tito
was as inspired by his men as they were by him. During a
nineteen-hour march up and over Mt. Igman, one Partisan
carried a wounded comrade on his back for three hours without a rest. When horses loaded with machine guns slipped
into frozen streams, Partisans waded in and got them out.
They followed Tito's example, practiced since his boyhood,
of dismounting when taking horses uphill to conserve the
animals' strength.

The ragged army often went hungry in regions where
the people also were starving. Sometimes the Partisans kept
alive on walnuts, dried wild pears or barley. Tito told Black
Zujovic, "We simply *must* get the men decent food. The
barley only sprouts in their stomach. We've got to build up
strength for the long marches and maneuvers ahead of us!"

Another serious problem was typhus, spread through
the mountains by lice. Tito's medical corps painted slogans
on village walls—WASH YOUR LINEN, CUT YOUR HAIR, KEEP
FREE OF LICE, AVOID TYPHUS. Some overzealous squads
roamed villages with clippers, shearing off the hair of anyone they caught. Alarmed, some peasant women bolted
themselves into their homes. Rankovic finally ordered the
practice stopped.

He brought Tito some bad news. Andrija Hebrang, a key Partisan commander, had been wounded and arrested by Ustase detectives in Zagreb. They had trampled him, kicked him senseless, then taken him to a hospital chained hand and foot. Pavelic himself had questioned him to learn Tito's whereabouts. Enraged by Hebrang's defiance, Pavelic had ordered him sent to the Ustase prison at Nova Gradiska, where prisoners were starved and tortured to death in solitary confinement. Tito promptly ordered a Partisan ambush of the prison car en route. Hebrang was rescued in a surprise attack, and escaped to rejoin Tito in the mountains.

Tito's chief link with the outside world was Radio Moscow. Its broadcasts irritated him by persistently referring to Mihailovic as the leader of the Yugoslav Resistance, obviously a conciliatory gesture to Churchill and the Yugoslav Royalist government in London.

He radioed Moscow tirelessly begging for airdrops of badly needed automatic weapons, ammunition, medical supplies, explosives and clothing. Finally he received a vaguely worded promise that an airdrop was "a possibility in the near future." He sent a squad of Partisans under Mosa Pijade, his old mentor from Lepoglava Prison, to push through six-foot snowdrifts in a 5,000-foot climb up Mt. Durmitor. Here they waited night after night on a freezing plateau, straining for the sound of Russian aircraft, in order to fire straw pile signals to guide the airdrop. A whole month passed as Pijade and his men camped on Mt. Durmitor in vain.

"*Ne razumin,*" Tito muttered to Djilas. "I don't understand. I keep sending message after message to Grandpapa assuring him if he sends the help we need, I can put another hundred thousand men under arms. He just keeps saying he'll see what can be done—or doesn't even mention help at all!"

Grandpapa was the Partisan code name for Joseph

Stalin; the messages were usually worded and sent by Dmitrov.

"Maybe we're looking for help in the wrong place," suggested Djilas wryly. "Why not ask Roosevelt?" It was after Pearl Harbor, and the United States was now a war ally against the Axis powers.

"Because Churchill has told him it's the Chetniks who are the real Resistance here. And Grandpapa lets them both go on believing it. It's ridiculous!"

"It's dialectics, Comrade." Djilas shrugged. "Stalin can't let the West think he's backing a revolutionary movement in Yugoslavia instead of the King's man, Mihailovic. They might get worried about world revolution and hold back the war supplies the Soviet Union needs."

Grandpapa himself confirmed Djilas' analysis in a radio message to Tito on March 5, 1942. Stalin criticized the formation of Proletarian Brigades; Churchill now suspected Russia of trying to Sovietize Yugoslavia. Tito must stop fighting Mihailovic and cooperate with the Chetniks instead. Partisan tactics were putting a strain on relations between the USSR and the Western Allies. As for Tito's charge that the Chetniks were collaborating with the Germans . . . nonsense! "There must be some great misunderstanding here," Stalin insisted. Tito and Djilas exchanged glances.

"There's a great misunderstanding, all right," Djilas said sarcastically. "But it's in the Kremlin!"

~~~~~~6

"Do Your
Utmost to Help Us!"

THE Third Enemy Offensive, March to June, 1942, forced
Tito out of Foca into the Zlatar Mountains of Montenegro,
pressed hard by overwhelming Italian forces supported by
Chetniks. "We must mercilessly destroy these bloodthirsty
men as they would destroy us," Mihailovic declared in orders
to his commanders in the field.

Tito fought fierce rear-guard actions as he withdrew.
His orders called for "swift, surprise assaults, night forays,
surrounding the enemy and regularly attacking him in the
rear. . . . A booty of weapons and ammunition must be the
result of each action." His supply of arms was dangerously
low.

He radioed Stalin desperately, "Soldiers and civilians
are asking why the Soviet Union does not send us aid, even
if only automatic weapons and ammunition. Our Partisans
are fighting with unprecedented heroism. . . . For us the
question of help is extremely serious. . . . The enemy is
making every effort to annihilate us."

"It is simply impossible to get supplies to you," Stalin

replied, and ironically suggested that Tito try appealing to the Royal Yugoslav Government in London.

On June 22, 1942, with food so low that the Partisans took to dynamiting trout in rivers, Tito made a desperate decision. If they stayed in the barren Zlatar Mountains they would either starve to death or be wiped out. He decided to break out of the enemy encirclement at all costs, spearing north through the rugged mountains of Bosnia to the Bosnian-Croatian border. The whole countryside here was seething with fury at the excesses of Pavelic and his Ustase, who were burning whole villages and massacring the inhabitants. Tito knew this region would place its entire resources at his disposal to attack the Ustase army.

He led the Partisans north in a drenching downpour that helped cloak their escape, following the border between the German and Italian zones of occupation. After an exhausting ten-day march on almost empty stomachs, they came to a deserted village that had apparently been wiped out by the Germans. Discovering twenty-five gallons of milk, Tito ordered it distributed only among the wounded. "For us," he told the others, "there is a whole mountain of wild strawberries!"

They found other villages untouched by the enemy, but with barely enough food to keep the peasants there alive.

"We must not take or ask for food here," Tito told his commanders grimly. "We'll capture it elsewhere. Meanwhile tell your men to talk less about our lack of food and concentrate on fighting the Germans. They won't feel so hungry!"

With his forces close to starvation, he led a desperate night attack across a bridge against a Ustase garrison at Bradina. Taken by surprise, the Ustase fled in panic. Some tried to escape with a loaded goods train. But as it began moving out of the garrison station, Partisans jumped aboard, overpowering the engineer and Ustase guards.

Tito's lined face broke out in a happy smile as his men

proudly showed him their prize—carloads of food, clothing, motorcycles, oil and half a ton of dynamite. Stripping the train and garrison of all supplies, Tito fed his starving army. The happy Partisans, finding some violins in Utsase barracks, struck up gay music. In the middle of the night men and women troops celebrated their victory with jubilant songs and dances.

Tito used the captured dynamite to blow up the train, tracks, tunnel, bridge and garrison. Then bellies full, wearing new boots and coats, freshly armed and supplied, the Partisans speared on northward, driving herds of sheep before them. When their captured caches of food ran out, they lived on lean, boiled mutton. No longer seeking only escape and survival, they sought out new enemy targets.

Tito's attacks on several other Ustase garrisons brought German divisions racing into Bosnia; but whenever they reached an outpost under attack, the Partisans had vanished.

Fighting his way north for four months, Tito finally reached the Bosnian-Croatian border. When he swooped down on the enemy garrison at Bihac, he found it commanded by none other than his World War I captain, Tomasevic, now a Ustase general notorious for mass atrocities against civilians. Tito captured the base in a fierce two-day battle, but Tomasevic escaped and was not captured until 1945, when he was executed for collaborating with the Germans.

Making Bihac his new headquarters, Tito dug in for the winter to consolidate his position and prepare to go on the offensive in 1943. Recruits flocked into Partisan ranks by the thousands. No longer a ragtag band of guerrilla fighters, they became a proud "National Army of Liberation"—two corps and eight divisions, 150,000 strong.

The time had come, Tito now told Kardelj and the others, to create a national Partisan government to control the areas his new army liberated. He radioed Moscow his intention to set up a National Liberation Committee. But Stalin, who had yet to put so much as a cartridge in Tito's hands, still regarded Yugoslavia primarily as a pawn in his own political chess game with the West.

The goal of a Red Yugoslavia was small potatoes to the Russian leader, who at the upcoming Teheran Conference with Churchill and Roosevelt needed to reassure—and disarm—them about his postwar intentions. He ordered Tito not to characterize the Liberation Committee as any kind of government or republic. It must be a broad united front coalition, not a YCP politburo. Under no circumstances must Tito challenge the authority of King Peter's government in exile!

Chafing, but still loyal to Moscow, Tito called for all patriotic groups in Yugoslavia to send delegates to his Anti-Fascist Council of National Liberation (AVNOJ) at Bihac on November 27, 1942. Several hundred delegates came— from the Croat Peasant Party, from Resistance newspapers in Slovenia and Dalmatia, from the Serb Democratic Party, from gun- and sword-toting mountaineers in Montenegro, from Moslem unions in Bosnia, from Orthodox Church groups in Serbia, from Partisan detachments fighting in every province.

Tito welcomed them in a speech intended to orient them toward Moscow, rather than toward London or Washington.

"All that we have hitherto achieved, Comrades," he declared, "is due first and foremost to our great Slav brother, Russia. . . . It was only our faith, our deep faith, in the strength and might of the Soviet Union and the Red Army which has sustained us and made us strong enough to overcome the trials of the last eighteen months."

He thanked them for civilian support of the Partisans: "Just look at all the razed villages. Homeless peasants, men and women, live in the freezing cold, in shacks, underneath the open sky, in the woods around a fire. But they do not bewail their fate. They say, 'Fight, dear brothers, and we will give you our last crust if it will help you to beat the common enemy.' Morale like that is rarely seen—something that the Yugoslav peoples can be proud of!"

He urged AVNOJ to new heroic efforts of supply: "Our army needs clothing, and we have no clothing factories. Our army needs weapons, and we have no arms factories. Our army needs food." He said nothing of his appeals to Moscow.

Delegates were stirred to tears by stories of Ustase atrocities related by mountain people. One old Serb peasant described how all in his village had been gathered in the schoolhouse, bound with ropes and divided into categories —those whose throats were to be cut; those to be thrown into pits and dispatched with grenades; girls and women to be violated, then pushed under river ice; children to be smashed to death against rocks or impaled on hay forks. The old peasant who had survived to tell of this dreadful event had been left for dead in a pit, but had only been badly wounded.

One Partisan reported his conversation with a captured Ustase who had told him about a "trick" learned from Italian Blackshirts—killing ten prisoners with one bullet: "You put the victims one behind the other, and then level their heads with a plank. If one sticks out a bit, a tap with a hammer will soon bring him down, and so you get a straight row of heads. Then with a shot into the nape of one man, you do all ten. That's a great saving."

Some delegates openly wept. Representing all racial, religious and social groups from all parts of the country, they joined in a solemn oath with Tito under homemade flags of the Soviet Union, Britain and the United States. They pledged to liberate Yugoslavia from the Axis invaders; to respect private property and freedom of enterprise; to punish only active collaborationists; to avoid atrocities; to guarantee the equal rights of all Yugoslav nationalties.

Later, at a private caucus of Partisan commanders, Black Zujovic grunted, "So you've slowed your fight for Socialism to suit Comrade Stalin. But what does he do for *you*?"

Tito looked reproachful. "*Molim vas.* Please—we would not be Partisans at all except for Moscow. What I have achieved was the work of the Party. I was an inexperienced young man when the Party took me under its wing, educated me and brought me up. I owe everything to it. All of us do. We must trust Grandpapa to know what he's doing!"

When the AVNOJ Conference broke up, the Partisans mounted their horses camouflaged with branches and rode back through pines weighed down by snow to their field headquarters in a forest cave. That night, huddled around a fire in the vast mountain darkness, they listened to a BBC radio news announcer report that the British War Office had authorized General Mihailovic to decorate 30 Chetniks in Yugoslavia for bravery in a guerrilla attack that had left 500 German dead.

"*Liar!*" Rankovic exploded. His boot lashed out, and the radio went flying against a wall of the cave.

Tito sighed. "How can you be so impractical, Marko?"

On December 5, 1942, he called a conference of women patriots, anti-Fascists and Partisans from all over Yugoslavia. Addressing them at Petrovac, he thanked them not only for being magnificent fighters but also for an indispensable supply corps. Thanks to them, every man in the Proletarian Brigade had uniforms, socks, coats and gloves. But more were needed: "These things depend mostly on you, our women comrades." He promised them complete equality with men in a postwar Yugoslavia: "You have more than earned it by shedding your blood, too, in combat on the battlefield."

To stiffen their resolve, he told them about an old peasant woman in the village of Kordum, captured by the Partisans from the Ustase. When some Ustase had been tried for atrocities and led off for execution, the old woman had flung herself upon them, screaming wildly as she beat and clawed their faces. After the rifle shots rang out, she had danced insanely in the blood of their bodies.

"Do not condemn her too harshly, Comrades," Tito told the women quietly. "The Ustase had slaughtered all her six sons in cold blood—for the crime of being Serbs."

As 1943 opened, Rommel's Nazi forces in North Africa were threatened with annihilation, exposing the German flank in southern Europe to Allied invasion. Hitler knew that Churchill was urging Stalin and Roosevelt to agree to landings in Yugoslavia. Alarmed and enraged, Hitler ordered Tito's Partisan army wiped out swiftly and completely, to prevent their use in support of an Adriatic invasion.

German General Alexander von Lohr hastily mounted Operation Weiss—the Fourth Enemy Offensive by Partisan count—designed to put an end to the exasperating and elusive Tito once and for all. On January 15, 1943, German Stukas swept out of the wintry sky, bombing and strafing Partisan units in the Grmec Mountains. Long-range artillery blasted the thick woods of the beech forest above Vrbinica.

Four Nazi divisions closed in from the north and east. The Italian Fifth Corps attacked from the West. The Chetniks took up positions to cut off any escape route to the south. The German plan was to encircle Tito and the Particans completely, strangle him slowly in a tightening noose, then destroy him with bombs and artillery.

There was no panic in Partisan ranks. The guerrillas took their cue from Tito, who remained, calm, cool, even well-groomed under all stress. At the darkest moments the thinning, pale and exhausted Partisan leader insisted upon remaining as clean-shaven and neat as field conditions permitted.

"It calms and encourages the men," he told his slim peasant wife Herta who, like all women Partisans, carried a heavy pack over battle dress, "to see their commander shaved and groomed no matter how tough the Germans make it for us!"

Marko Rankovic urged him to escape to a safe hideout near Zagreb, and conduct operations from there. "For the sake of the movement. We can't afford to lose you!"

"Nonsense," Tito replied scornfully. "Any one of you could take my place. If I have any value to the cause at all, it is here in the field with the men, under fire."

Kardelj smiled dryly. "Tell the truth, Comrade Tito. You *enjoy* the dangers of matching wits with the Fascists!"

Tito realized that the enemy had located the field headquarters he had established in the forest above Vrbinica when German planes suddenly screamed low overhead, dropping a stick of bombs. *Whoomp!* He, Djilas, Rankovic and Zujovic automatically flung themselves to earth.

Whoomp-whoomp-whoomp! A black-smoked blast of dirt, steel and stones cascaded over them. They remained motionless as another Luftwaffe plane swooped down and emptied its load. When the engine throb faded in the bleak winter sky, Tito rose. Wryly examining a large slash ripped in his battle jacket by a bomb fragment, he anxiously watched the other three members of the Partisan general staff lift themselves from the soggy floor of the beech forest.

"Everybody all right?" he asked hopefully.

Black Zujovic's saturnine features were dark with dismay. "That was pinpoint bombing. Someone is a traitor!"

"We've got to break out of here," Milovan Djilas insisted. "To wait any longer means annihilation!"

Tito paced restlessly up and down in front of their shelter, lost in thought. Ideas formed with each step.

"We'll fight our way south across the Neretva River."

Kardelj stared at him. "*Nemoguche!* Impossible! We have three thousand sick and wounded. We can't leave them behind!"

"Everybody has to take his chances," Rankovic snapped. He had spent six years in jail at hard labor, had been tortured, had seen his wife outraged and killed by the Nazis.

Kardelj shook his head. "You don't understand, Comrade. It's physically impossible. How could we get them across the river under the guns of the Chetniks? And then over the passes of the Neretva in the freezing cold and snow?"

"Let them fight their way out with us!"

Tito nodded grimly. "Rankovic is right. It's the only way. Arm every man—wounded or not. Put those with light wounds in one battalion. We'll make a cavalry battalion out of wounded men who can still ride. Only the worst cases will go on stretchers—but *also* as a fighting battalion!"

The forest came alive as Tito gave the signal to move out. Fighting columns headed south, single file. Tito watched them grimly, well aware they would be lucky if as many as a third got through the German trap alive. Daily air attacks were only part of the Partisan ordeal. Food was once more dangerously low. There were not enough horses for even the seriously wounded to ride. Typhus was still endemic, with a heartbreaking shortage of drugs, bandages and medics. Bitter winds froze the marchers as they struggled through huge, shoulder-high snowdrifts and ice-fringed torrents.

"They'll die like flies before we even get to the Neretva River," Zujovic muttered at Tito's side as they pressed into the winter gales. "It would have been more merciful to the wounded to leave them behind!"

"To fall into the hands of the Ustase or Germans? At

least this way they escape torture with a fighting chance!"

Tito saw a plane swoop low over a column in the ice-crusted woodlands, spraying a gray cloud. *"Poison gas!"*

The men broke ranks and dived for safety. But the cloud proved to be simply a drop of propaganda leaflets promising safe conduct and pardon if the Partisans laid down their arms and surrendered. A guerrilla captain brought copies to Tito and Zujovic. Cocking a captured Luger in his hand, he asked, "Shall I kill any man who pockets one?"

Tito shook his head. "No, Comrade. Encourage the men to collect as many as possible. They're nice and thin. And we're terribly short of cigarette and toilet paper!"

For ten straight days, refusing to call a halt, he led the Partisan columns through the frozen heights of the Grmec Mountains. Struggling beside his men through huge snowdrifts, he grew chilled in the same threadbare uniform; shared the same hunger. When they were not stumbling through blizzards, they were dodging swarms of German and Italian planes that filled the skies whenever they turned blue.

Six divisions under General von Lohr pressed in from west, north and east. Tito slowed them down, deploying rear-guard thrusts by hit-and-run Partisan forces on his periphery. But his own 125-mile thrust to the Neretva River was severely crippled by the snail's pace required by his insistence upon evacuating the wounded.

He kept firing hopeful radio messages to Moscow, begging for supplies. He told Stalin that the enemy was jeering at them as "five-bullet men"—because that was all the ammunition Tito could spare for each Partisan.

"Is it really impossible," he implored, "after twenty months of heroic, almost superhuman fighting, to find some way of helping us? . . . People are dying like flies from starvation, yet do not complain. These starving people give our fighting men their last crust, while they themselves die like flies. They give their last sock, shirt or boot, and go barefoot themselves in midwinter. Do your utmost to help us!" The reply from Grandpapa came ten days later:

"You must not for an instant doubt that, if there were the least possibility of giving you any material help in your wonderful, heroic struggle, we should long ago have done so. . . . The moment it is possible, we shall do all we can. Can you doubt that? Try to understand!"

Tito tried. He understood . . . only too well.

7

Crisis
at the Neretva

HE KNEW now that all he could ever expect from Moscow was flowery best wishes, despite the six Nazi divisions he was tying down that could otherwise be hurled against the Soviet front. But he fought off gnawing doubts. It was simply unthinkable that the sacred cause to which he had devoted his whole life—international Communism—would betray him. If he lost faith in Stalin, what would be left to believe in?

Each day of the retreat brought a fresh toll of wounded, sick and dying. Succumbing to exposure, hunger and exhaustion, hundreds of Partisans stumbling along on sticks or crutches sank into the deep snow and fell behind as grim trail markers of the exodus. When morning sun melted the night's icy snow crust, horses loaded with packs sank through. Men had to carry field guns on their own backs.

Tito narrowly escaped death on several occasions. Once a Nazi bomb scored a direct hit on a mountain hut in which he was poring over maps. Lodging in a beam directly over his head, it failed to explode. Weeks later an Italian reconnaissance party discovered his field headquarters in a Serbian peasant cottage at Drenova. He had just arisen from sleep on the floor, bag for pillow, coat for blanket.

"Soldiers coming!" Zujovic yelled from the window.

Zujovic and several Partisans sprinted out a rear door with all papers and a radio transmitter. Seizing submachine guns, Tito and two men ran out the front and opened fire from behind trees to cover Zujovic's escape. The Italians replied with mortar and machine-gun fire.

The peasant's family fled with Tito and his men, including two babies born just hours before the attack. A Partisan carried them off in his coat. The Italians fired the cottage, burning to death the babies' mother who could not leave or be moved.

Tito had, as his English translator and private secretary, a daughter of one of the King's ministers-in-exile. Olga Nincic, a tall, well-built, brunette Partisan, wore black beeches, boots and a pistol at her belt. One day she ran into headquarters with tragic news. Ustase commandos had attacked a training camp for Partisan women, killing many and taking prisoners for torture and interrogation.

One instructor captured was Herta, Tito's wife. He immediately sent word to General von Lohr that he was willing to exchange some high-ranking officers he held prisoner for the Partisan women. Von Lohr agreed.

Arranging the exchange under a flag of truce, Vladko Velebit, one of Tito's commanders, asked his opposite number, General von Horstenau, if the Germans would agree to recognize the rights of Partisans as combatants, with a restriction on both sides against killing wounded prisoners.

Von Horstenau made a counterproposal: that the Partisans join the Germans in opposing any Allied landing on the Dalmatian coast. When this was reported to Berlin, Hitler reproached von Horstenau: "You don't negotiate with rebels; you shoot them!" His propaganda minister, Goebbels, saw a chance to create mischief and undermine Partisan prestige. He spread the word that Tito had entered into negotiations with the Germans to try to arrange an armistice.

Moscow immediately radioed sharp questions. When Tito explained, the Kremlin criticized him for having negotiated the prisoner exchange. At this he lost his temper.

"Our first duty is to look after our army and our own people," he radioed back angrily. "If you cannot understand what a difficult time we are having, and if you cannot help us, at least do not hinder us!"

Tito's forces continued to press ahead toward Prozor, where a garrison of about a thousand Italians blocked passage across the Neretva River. Time was urgent. If General von Lohr realized his plan, the German 717th Division would be rushed east to close the Partisans' only chance to escape south.

"I think we've got to mislead Von Lohr at all costs," he told his staff. "He probably knows our advance units are already across the Neretva. But he might think we've changed our minds if we pull them back over the bridge at Jablonica, and then blow it up."

Edvard Kardelj stared at him in disbelief. "That's mad! Why blow up the bridge when we need it to cross?"

But Zujovic understood and chuckled. "Tito's right! The Germans will think we're going to dig in and fight on *this* side of the river. We help them think that with attacks on Prozor and Konjic. Von Lohr will rush the 717th to relieve them. Meanwhile . . ." He grinned at Tito.

Tito nodded. "Meanwhile our engineers will throw up a makeshift bridge across the Neretva. And we'll cross while our Third Division keeps the Germans busy!"

"*Opasnost,*" Rankovic muttered. "Dangerous. We could lose two thirds of our men in a bottleneck like that!"

"It's our only chance," Tito said grimly.

Despite a gauntlet of bombs, shells and flank attacks,

they reached the outskirts of Prozor by February 15, 1943. Tito's advance echelon, on the other side of the Neretva, returned across the Jablonica bridge and blew it up behind them. Chetnik observers, watching through glasses from the top of Mt. Prenj, promptly radioed this "retreat" to German field headquarters. Then Tito made his second feint.

He sent his Third Division against the Italian-held garrison of Prozor; his Second to take the towns of Imotski and Jablonica, which were protected by another Italian division; his First to besiege Konjic, a mixed garrison strongly held by Germans, Italians and Chetniks. Blazing fighting broke out all along the north side of the Neretva.

The Second Division quickly took their objective. The Third ran into heavy artillery fire and mortars. Two tanks rumbled out of the Prozor garrison, blazing away at the charging Partisans, hundreds of whom fell on the snowy slope. But when Tito's men overran Prozor, the Italians, who had no appetite for hand-to-hand combat, quickly surrendered.

Howitzers captured at Prozor were rushed to help the First Division, which was meeting fierce opposition at Konjic. Visiting this front, Tito found his artillerymen perspiring in the freezing night. They ran constantly with heavy shells to keep the howitzers blazing until they were red-hot, their flashes lighting up the dark mountains.

General Robotti, Commander of the Italian Second Army, sent a frantic SOS to General von Lohr: "For God's sake, undertake immediate measures to relieve the pressure on our forces!" Von Lohr rushed the 718th German Division from Sarajevo to Robotti's rescue, and dispatched the 717th to attack the Partisans now holding Prozor.

Black Zujovic was delighted. "It worked!"

"I'll keep the Germans busy, Black," Tito said. "You get a rough bridge up over the Neretva and start crossing."

In the first clashes with the advancing Germans, the Partisans took some prisoners. One was a Nazi lieutenant colonel whose large German wolfhound, Luz, Tito admired and "liberated." The German officer was amazed when he saw fifteen tanks and heavy artillery in Partisan hands.

"Do you mean to tell me," he demanded of Tito, "that you hauled all of that with you through the mountains?"

"No. It was donated by your Italian allies up here."

"Oh, the sweet Italians!" the Nazi colonel snarled.

Tito established field headquarters in a rough gray stone shack near a little water mill above the Neretva. He ordered the Third Division to attack the advancing German 718th furiously, as though trying to break through to the north to escape. The more cautious and defensive he could make the Nazis, the more time Zujovic would have to build his bridge and start the Partisan flight south.

Every hour counted. Tito knew that as soon as Von Lohr realized he had been tricked, Stukas would roar overhead, bombing unmercifully as the Partisans attempted to force their way across the river. And the survivors would still have to fight their way up the jagged limestone crags of Mt. Prenj, over 7,000 feet high, covered by ice and snow and defended by 14,000 Chetnik troops in fortified positions on every peak.

"It may safely be said," Tito wrote later, "that the destiny of our revolution was decided at the Neretva River."

On the evening of March 6, 1943, he stood next to the water mill, staring down with Djilas and Zujovic at the wild torrents below, now eighty yards wide and turbulent with the melting snows of early spring. Partisan engineers, tied together by ropes, were threading a narrow plank bridge through the twisted girders of the railroad bridge that had been blown up and now lay half in, half out of the river.

Harassing fire came from a camouflaged blockhouse in a canyon wall on the opposite side of the river. Tito studied it for a few moments through binoculars.

"That's a job for volunteers," he told Zujovic. "Six men with hand grenades and submachine guns."

Shortly before dawn six guerrillas of the Second Dalmatian Brigade crawled, groped and fought across the churning rapids. Weaving in and out of the bridge girders, they silently climbed the steep canyon wall beneath the blockhouse. At a signal from the squad leader, they hurled grenades at the small window. Two explosions rocked the pillbox. The commandos scrambled inside, submachine guns blazing.

Then they retreated to the river bank to stand guard while Partisan engineers worked in the first dim light of the awakening sky to rush completion of the crude bridge. Tito and Zujovic inspected the rickety structure over which 25,-000 soldiers and wounded men would have to cross.

"Think we can get any heavy stuff across, Black?"

"*Nemoguche.* Impossible."

Tito looked mournful. "We went to a lot of trouble taking it away from the Italians."

Shrugging, Zujovic pointed to the top of Mt. Prenj.

"We can get more from the Chetniks up there."

Reluctantly, Tito ordered all tanks, trucks and heavy artillery jettisoned. The Partisans tipped them over down the steep slope, watching the spectacle as they crashed heavily into the narrow gorge of the Neretva, strewing the river with huge, twisted debris.

"Start the crossing!" Tito commanded.

Long columns began to move down the steep slippery slope. Wounded men crawled down on all fours. Some were so enfeebled by typhus that they plunged down the mountain, unable to check, hurtling headlong into the foaming river to drown. Packhorses also fell and slipped into the churning waters.

Men who could walk helped carry those who could not. Tired, sick and hungry, they dragged themselves down to the crude bridge and across it. Many of the wounded cavalry, trying to swim their own mounts across, were carried away in the swirling rapids. Italian prisoners, carrying their wounded on stretchers, cursed and shook their fists at their Chetnik allies when bursts of mortar fire came from the heights of Mt. Prenj. Some balked at crossing the river under fire. Partisan commanders cooly shot them on the spot.

"Keep that line moving!" The cry echoed persistently up and down the north bank of the Neretva, as anxious eyes studied the sky for the first German Stukas.

Fresh casualties poured in from the fighting lines of the Third Division, led by Marko Rankovic, which was buying time with blood. The crossing went on all night.

When a pale blue dawn broke through the valley, Tito's bloodshot eyes grew foreboding in the sunrise. "Flying weather. What do you think, Black? Should we continue crossing in daylight? Or hide until tonight?"

"We haven't that much time," Zujovic replied. "Rankovic and his men can't hold off Von Lohr much longer."

The first Stukas came swarming over the surrounding hills at 10:45 A.M. Flight after flight. One by one they peeled off and swooped down on open targets. Bombs roared down on Jablonica, the Partisan-held town above the Neretva, making it a ruin of bodies, horses and rubble.

German pilots strafed the columns of wounded moving down one slope, over the bridge, and up the foothills of Mt. Prenj. The valley and steep slopes on both sides rocked with explosions, flame and smoke making the peaks seem like volcanoes erupting. Some planes flew low, skip-bombing the bridge. As often as they knocked out a section, Partisan engineers rushed to patch it up. Tito watched grimly as the Neretva turned red with the blood of his followers.

It seemed incredible that any of them would escape with their lives. Standing on top of the slope, Tito did not flinch as a Stuka swooped by, strifing close to him.

"If Stalin had only sent a few antiaircraft guns!" he

said bitterly to Zujovic. There had been none to capture; the Germans had not needed protection from the air.

They watched grimly as a pony lost its footing on the slippery planks and plunged into the raging waters. A narrow miss by a bomb jarred the bridge. Some of the wounded, thrown down by the blast, crawled the rest of the way on all fours. Tito turned away, blinded by tears.

Later in the afternoon Rankovic returned from the front to confer with Tito and Zujovic on the best way to disengage the Third Division from their battle with the German 718th without endangering the crossing. As they deliberated, Rankovic watched the Stukas dive-bombing long lines of wounded men being carried on stretchers. He choked up.

"The dogs! No, Comrades, we won't withdraw until the last man of you here is across—even if we all die!"

The crossing of the Neretva took a full week. On some days the bombing and strafing were so intense that Tito was forced to order a halt to crossings until dark. Finally, on March 10, he crossed over himself, climbing up to the foothills of Mt. Prenj to set up a new headquarters.

Only then did Rankovic fall back to the bridge, fighting a delaying action. When the Third Division ran short of grenades, they began hurling rocks. Surviving Partisans raced across the river on March 15, once more blowing up the bridge, this time in the faces of their Nazi pursuers.

As Tito and the main force advanced up the vast crags of Mt. Prenj, the dug-in Chetniks opened up with artillery, mortars and machine-gun crossfire. Italian Savoias appeared in the sky twenty feet over the climbers' heads. Tito waved his men to cover in an adjacent forest.

Over a thousand men were caught in a narrow track between two peaks, unable to move left or right because of deep snow, blocked ahead by a column of wounded men and typhus cases. Shrapnel shells exploded among the column, inflicting terrible casualties. A rain of mortars probed the forest for Tito and the main force as they climbed toward the heavily fortified positions of the Chetniks above.

But the 14,000 Royalist troops proved to be the weakest link in the Axis chain. Many had had enough of collaboration with the enemy against fellow Yugoslavs. Those who had joined Mihailovic expecting to fight the Fascist invaders of their country were frequently bewildered to find themselves attacking Partisans instead. Now one Chetnik gun-pit after another went over to Tito's forces. Some had already shaved off their traditional beards and long hair in preparation. Thousands of Chetniks panicked and fled into Montenegro. Mihailovic never recovered from the debacle.

On top of Mt. Prenj, Tito stared around him bitterly. The Fourth Enemy Offensive, like the other three, had failed. Weakened by hunger, sickness, wounds and exhaustion, the Partisans had escaped Hitler's trap once more. But the cost had been terrible. Fewer than half of his followers had survived. Some who had were even now sitting down in the snow and dying, their hearts having given out.

And a long, agonizing journey still lay ahead.

The German failure to destroy the Partisans left Hitler beside himself with rage. Heads began rolling among the Nazi General Staff. Still fearful of an Allied invasion through Yugoslavia, he screamed new orders to wipe Tito and his men out as a fighting force immediately, regardless of cost.

Two months later 120,000 Axis troops—outnumbering the Partisans ten to one—began to forge a new ring of steel around Tito's position on the border of Montenegro and Bosnia in mountainous canyon country. His three divisions, now down to less than 20,000 men in all, were ragged and war-weary, while the Germans had seven fresh divisions specially trained for mountain warfare.

Worse, Von Lohr had finally learned the lessons that Tito's brilliant guerrilla warfare had taught. He began to deploy his troops to fight flexibly, guerrilla style. They

encircled the Partisans with little fortresses of stone and
steel from which they struck in commando force. They laid
ambushes. They used trained dogs to discover Partisans positions and to pursue Tito's men when they hit and ran.

Mountain peasants were mobilized as carriers. Their
horses and food stocks were confiscated, to cut the Partisans off from their only source of supply and make it easier
for Nazi troops to live in the mountains. Von Lohr also reinforced his men by airdropping fresh troops, along with arms
and supplies, wherever they were needed.

Tito's position had never been more desperate. He ordered fresh radio contact made with Moscow.

Djilas checked the radio log. "This makes your seventy-
third appeal since we started fighting," he said dryly. "Well,
you can say one thing about Grandpapa. He's consistent!"

Tito radioed Stalin hopefully: "We request your help
in this supreme trial. If you do not airdrop arms, medical
supplies and food to us now, we are lost!" The reply from
the Kremlin praised the Partisans as glorious heroes of the
Revolution, encouraged them to continue their magnificent
struggle against Fascism, and expressed "deepest regrets"
that it was just not possible to send them help at this time.

Two days later Zujovic reported they were out of food.

"We can probably subsist for a few days on beech
leaves, sorrel and garlic," he said. "But we've got to break
out."

The embattled Partisan leader studied his maps gloomily. "Our best chance of escape is south toward Foca. Send
the First Division to probe enemy defenses there."

But the German net of steel proved just as strong around
Foca as at other points. The Partisan First Division was flung
back with ruinous losses. There was more bad news in a
directive taken off the body of a Nazi captain.

Tito read it aloud grimly to his staff: "Every Partisan
found is to be shot. If the local inhabitants are hostile to

the German forces, treat them with the greatest possible brutality and severity. If they are friendly, harness them in the struggle against the Partisans. Destroy anything that could be of the slightest use to Partisan forces. Foul all water supplies."

Edvard Kardelj shook his head glumly. "If they're able to cut us off from the people, it will be our finish!"

Their plight grew hopeless as twelve Axis divisions tightened their ring around Tito's position. He decided that their only chance lay in swift, unimpeded flight.

"Smash and conceal all heavy armaments," he told Zujovic. "Give permission for the men to eat their horses."

Rankovic brought word that Von Lohr was rushing divisions along their flanks. "Well, that settles it," he sighed. "We'll have to try fighting through in the south."

"No," said Tito.

"No? But there's nowhere else for us to go!"

"Oh, yes, there is. Where they least expect us. Where they've already repulsed us. We're attacking north *again!*"

8

"We Can't Believe You're Still Alive!"

PARTISANS ambushed a Nazi reconnaissance party, and a search of prisoners revealed a German order dated May 29, 1943. Djilas brought it to Tito, who read:

"When the ring is completely closed, the Communists will make individual attempts to break through. Therefore it is ordered that not one male capable of fighting shall be allowed to escape alive from the ring. All women are to be examined to make sure they are not disguised males."

"The Nazi mind in flower," Tito said sarcastically.

A British laison officer, who had been landed by submarine in Montenegro as an observer, told Tito in astonishment, "We had information that you were fighting the Germans, but we never believed there were battles like these, or that the Germans would be obliged to throw in so many divisions against you!" His enthusiastic report reached General Harold Alexander, in command of the British Forces Middle East, who sent Tito a message of encouragement: "Hang on! The Second Front is not a dream. Your struggle will gain in significance in the coming months."

On June 8, 1943, Tito led a mounted reconnaissance party of two hundred men north up Mt. Milinklada. The Germans were dug in less than three miles away. Dusk and rainfall covered their advance, but the Nazis opened fire. One shell burst squarely on the column, killing a dozen Partisans. The rest scattered. Thick mist blotted out one mounted guerrilla from another. Tito, finding himself alone, groped through the wet grass until he finally made contact with a squad.

Re-forming the battalion, he led it up to the summit of Mt. Milinklada, where they camped for the night. The morning dawned dry and sunny. Suddenly a few Stukas and Dorniers swooped low overhead, bombing and strafing. Tito's bodyguard and six others nearby were blown to bits. At the first sound of explosions, Tito threw himself face down.

Antipersonnel shrapnel flying at his head hit, instead, the wolfhound, Luz, stretched at his side. Tito was wounded in his left arm. Stunned, his dazed glance fell on a shattered tree adjacent, where a small mountain bird, one of its legs torn off by the blast, stood on the other complaining plaintively. Bleeding profusely, Tito ignored his injury as he led the battalion back to headquarters.

While his wound was being bandaged, he admitted to Zujovic that a direct breakout through the Nazi encirclement was hopeless. Wherever they had probed, they had been hurled back by fierce counterattacks. The noose was being drawn tighter. "There's only one chance, Black. Straight up the Maglich Massif. From the top we'll fight through to the northwest, wherever the Nazi lines are thinnest."

Zujovic whistled. "Up the *Maglich*! But it's four thousand feet practically straight up! Is it possible?"

"*Ne*. No—so Partisans will do it anyhow!"

The First Proletarian Brigade, the oldest guerrilla unit with the best fighting record, led the assault on Maglich.

They forced their way up almost perpendicular limestone cliffs to the towering alp, whose craggy pinnacles stabbed at the sky. It was a bare, rocky region where the peasants seldom could raise enough to feed themselves.

Thin and pale, Tito climbed up using his right arm, the other immobilized in a sling. Like his men he was close to starvation, his rugged strength sapped. As they reached the top of the Maglich, he saw some men become delirious. One Partisan pointed to a tree, shouting, "A chimney!" A whole column raced behind him to the hallucinated warmth of a house and fireplace. One squad lined up numbly with mess tins in front of a snow bank, deluded by a sergeant who convinced them that it was a field kitchen serving hot food.

Stumbling with his men across the Maglich, Tito fought off slashing attacks on their flanks by Von Lohr's well-fed mountain divisions, who fell upon them like wolf packs.

Ghastly evidence of Nazi brutality was everywhere on their march to the northwest. The Germans had burned villages, killing thousands of peasants in reprisal for attacks on Nazi troops. One Dalmatian unit of Partisans found a cave filled with the bodies of fifty-two women and children. Miraculously, a one-year-old baby was found still alive among the dead. Tito ordered one of the women Partisans to treat the baby's wounds and carry it along with them.

As they struggled across the Maglich, they were joined by whole families of old men, and women and children fleeing from the Nazis. Their numbers increased daily until over 100,000 refugees were blocking the mountain paths, moving so slowly that the Partisan columns were in danger of bogging down. Barefoot, hungry, ill-clad and freezing, often unable to drag one foot after the other, a few lucky ones riding in ox-drawn wagons, they stumbled on with the soldiers. Many froze to death in the exposure of the bitter mountain nights, or starved.

"We've *got* to leave them behind!" Rankovic pleaded. "If we slow down any more, the Germans will have time to shift divisions and cut off our escape!"

Muscles pulsed in Tito's cheeks. "Are you *crazy*, Black? How could we leave our own people behind for the Germans to massacre? Who do you think we are—Ustase?"

A brace of long-range artillery shells crashed a thousand yards from their position, probing for the columns snaking through a snow-smothered pine forest. Rankovic growled, "All right, but for God's sake, hurry the people up!"

They stayed alive by killing and eating emaciated pack ponies, and afterward chewing beech leaves or distilling the juice of beech bark. A German prisoner they captured declared scornfully, "We have white bread, sausages and butter every day—while you survive on horseflesh and leaves!"

They pressed on across the Maglich despite the thud of mortars, crash of howitzer shells, rattle of machine-gun fire and blasts of Nazi bombers. Their heavy losses were aggravated by casualties who fell from hunger, sickness and infected wounds. But never did Tito or the Partisans consider surrender.

They were firmly convinced of the ultimate triumph of the forces of Socialism. It was inevitable. Marx had said it; Lenin had said it; Stalin had said it; Tito had said it. The fighters for a "people's democracy" had only to persevere, and victory would reward their great suffering. Besides, the Partisans knew only too well that Von Lohr had been ordered by Hitler to take no prisoners.

Tito kept them marching all night and some of the day until they could barely stay on their feet. Some moved as if in a dream, oblivious of cold, hunger and fatigue, indifferent to the bombs and shells that burst close by.

"The men can't last much longer," Zujovic warned.

Tito stabbed a calloused finger at a grimy map. "We'll break out here—the road between Kalinovik and Foca."

"But that's open valley! German artillery would tear us to pieces if they caught us on the plains!"

"Not if we run fast enough! Sure it's against all military strategy. That's just why Von Lohr doesn't expect us to be crazy enough to try it, and why it's bound to be the most lightly held position on the perimeter!"

A resolute figure in a plain dark tunic without badge of rank except the pistol on his hip, Tito went forward to talk to the men of the First Proletarian Brigade.

"I know you always fight well," he told them. "But this time I want you to fight as if you don't care whether you live or die. You might as well. If we can't punch a hole through the Second Battalion of the German 369th, we'll all be finished within two days. It's up to you!"

As night fell on June 12, 1943, they left their mountain concealment, descending into a vast open meadow. Spreading out, each man on his own, they charged across the valley at top speed. Met by a storm of shellfire, mortars and machine-gun crossfire from German troops dug in along the Kalinovik-Foca road, hundreds of Partisans fell. Others stumbled over their bodies and went down. But hundreds more charged over their bodies, screaming Yugoslav war cries.

The first shock wave of Partisans overran the Nazi gun emplacements. Bitter hand-to-hand struggles filled the dark valley with groans of the dying. In the fierce fighting almost half the attackers were killed. But a gap was torn through the defenses of the 369th German Division.

Dazed Nazis on the perimeter fell back. The whole First Partisan Division came pouring through the gap, followed by Tito leading the other two divisions and civilians.

The Germans counterattacked on both flanks as quickly as they could bring up fresh troops. But the incredible Partisans fought them off in a raging battle that lasted twenty-four hours. Those who survived staggered into the deep forest on the other side of the road. Behind them the trap closed again on most of the sick and wounded, Partisans as well as civilians. All were slaughtered mercilessly.

Peasants who lived in the forest stared incredulously at the spectacle of Tito's battle-weary, half-dead warriors who had smashed through the most dreaded military machine in the world. One old farmer caught sight of a sun- and snow-burned Partisan with iron-gray hair and hard lines of suffering around his hollow cheeks, and embraced him.

"I recognize you from your picture on the reward posters!" he laughed in delight. "It's impossible that you're still alive, Comrade Tito. The Chetniks have been telling everyone that the Germans wiped you all out!"

"They tried their best," Tito smiled wearily.

General von Lohr, humiliated by his latest and worst failure, sent an apologetic explanation to the outraged dictator of Nazi Germany: "The fighting was exceptionally heavy. All the commanders agreed that their troops were engaged in the most bitter struggle of the war. A ferocious Partisan attack effected a breakthrough near Miljevina. The enemy forces managed to retreat through the resulting gap and disappeared in the mountains to the north. We were too exhausted to stop them, and there were no reserves."

A guerrilla signalman picked up a radio message for Tito from Moscow. "We congratulate our brave Yugoslav comrades-in-arms for their new brilliant victory over the Fascist invaders," Stalin enthused. "Yours is a remarkable effort, which our Soviet land and all freedom-loving peoples will never forget. Keep up your heroic fight!"

Tito listened to Rankovic read it to him jubilantly as his wife Herta rebandaged his arm wound. Mouth grim as he thought of all the Yugoslav freedom fighters who lay dead for lack of food, medicine and ammunition, he said, "Reply to Comrade Stalin that we will try to mold bullets out of his best wishes, since we know now this is all he will ever send. And tell him he can go straight to ——"

His eyes met Rankovic's stricken gaze. "No, cancel that," he said wearily. "Just tell him that we're honored by his high opinion, and hope to continue to merit it."

By now the West was aware that the real mountain fighting in Yugoslavia was being led by a romantic popular hero named Tito, identified as a veteran revolutionist, Josip Broz. Reward posters all over occupied Yugoslavia offered 100,000 gold marks for his capture. But the elusive Partisan leader was too old a hand at living and fighting underground to be taken by surprise. His headquarters were usually a well-hidden hut, cave or branch lean-to, moved swiftly from place to place with an unerring instinct for danger.

Still blessed with an iron physique at fifty-one, he lived at a pace that made it hard for men half his age to keep up. In a single night he would march twenty miles to lead a guerrilla raid; melt away to breakfast at some village and discuss their problems with peasants; inspect a Partisan outpost; return to his headquarters for a meal; study maps and intelligence reports with Zujovic; play a game of chess or two with Djilas. When he lay down on some branches to sleep, he dozed lightly, ready to spring to his feet at a moment's notice and lead an escape.

The morale of his troops was always high, no matter how desperate the circumstances. His Partisans knew that if one of them was wounded, Tito would risk four or five men —including his own life—to rescue him. They took pride in his daring commando attacks against huge forces, counting on the element of surprise. When surrounded, they relied on his tactic of probing for the weakest point and escaping by breaking through it at top speed. In the moments of fiercest fighting, they knew they could always find him in the thick of it.

In London, Winston Churchill, apprised of the true situation in Yugoslavia, began to have second thoughts about the arms and supplies he was shipping to the Chetniks. It was Tito, obviously, and not the Royalist Mihailovic who had popular support and who was fighting the Germans.

True, Tito was a diehard Communist. But it was Stalin, not Tito, Churchill felt sure, who would determine the post-war government of Yugoslavia. And Stalin was proving co-operative with the West. On May 22, 1943, as a "gesture of friendship," the Kremlin boss had dissolved the Comintern, indicating that he no longer intended to export Communist revolution to other countries.

Reassured, Churchill decided to send a military mission to Tito. Accordingly, in July a group of British liaison officers led by Fitzroy Maclean, and later joined by the Prime Minister's own son, Randolph Churchill, parachuted into Tito's hideout in the mountains. Maclean became a part of Tito's headquarters. A political conservative like Churchill, he was nevertheless deeply impressed by what he saw.

Radioing London that Mihailovic was, indeed, "hope-lessly compromised in his relations with the Axis," Maclean warned, "Whether we help the Partisans or not, they will be the decisive political factor in Yugoslavia after the war." He pointed out that as long as England was helping the Com-munists in Russia to fight Hitler, it made no sense to refuse the same help to the Communists in Yugoslavia.

Maclean also hazarded the shrewd guess that Tito's intense nationalist feeling might well prevail over his Com-munist loyalties. In mid-1943, when even Tito would have hotly denied that he might ever place Belgrade before Mos-cow in his affections, that was a remarkable prediction.

The surrender of Italy on September 8, 1943, provided the Allies with their first opportunity to show Tito that they now considered him part of the team. The Allied Supreme Middle East Command ordered the Italian Army occupying Yugoslavia to surrender, not to Mihailovic, but to Tito. Many Italian units, eager to get out of a war forced on them by Mussolini's megalomania, eagerly turned themselves and their equipment over to the nearest Partisan units. Some not quick enough were seized by the Nazis and Chetniks.

That same month Hitler launched the Sixth Enemy Offensive. A huge Nazi onslaught drove the Partisans out of the positions in Slovenia and Dalmatia surrendered by the Italians. By January, 1944, only the coastal island of Vis remained held by combined British and Partisan forces. Tito eluded the pitched battles Von Lohr sought to force upon him, and escaped with his men into the mountains of Bosnia.

On the political front, meanwhile, the three Allied foreign ministers—Anthony Eden for London, Vyacheslav Molotov for Moscow, Cordell Hull for Washington—had met in Cairo with King Peter and a new prime minister, Bozidar Puric, to discuss the nature of a postwar Yugoslav government. Eden declared Britain's aim to be "a completely free Yugoslavia," with Peter on the throne. The ministers were startled to receive a radio message from Bosnia.

"We acknowledge neither the Yugoslav government nor the King abroad," Tito warned them, "because for two and a half years they have supported the enemy collaborator, the traitor Draza Mihailovic. We shall not let them return!"

At the Bosnian hill town of Jajce, Tito reassembled the Anti-Fascist Council of National Liberation (AVNOJ) he had set up a year earlier at Bihac. He told the delegates that the Allies were beginning to get quantities of military equipment and food to him, and expressed the hope that tanks and planes would follow. He condemned as slander all charges that the Partisans planned to seize power, bolshevize Yugoslavia, abolish private property and wipe out religion.

Delegates roared their approval of his proposal to declare the Royal Yugoslav Government null and void, replacing it with a National Committee of Liberation. Tito was elected Prime Minister, Minister of Defense and, a new distinction, Marshal of Yugoslavia.

It was no coincidence that the AVNOJ convention took

place at Jajce on November 26, 1943, the day before the Big Three were scheduled to meet at Teheran in Iran. Until now Yugoslavia had been regarded primarily as a military problem. Suddenly Tito had injected a new and potentially upsetting note into the deliberations at Teheran—the question: what kind of governments in Europe would succeed Hitler's puppet regimes, totalitarian or democratic?

Stalin was extremely annoyed at Tito. The war was not yet won. This was no time for a falling-out of the Allies!

But Tito's bold move was more succesful than he could have hoped. The Teheran Conference agreed that Mihailovic had to be officially repudiated and Tito supported. It made little practical difference whether Mihailovic had been motivated by sincere anti-Communist or pro-Royalist feelings, or was a traitor or opportunist. The blunt fact was that the common enemy was not Communism but Fascism, and collaborating with Fascists was treason to the Allied cause.

Tito wrote Churchill a reassuring letter that all he really wanted was a democratic and united Yugoslavia. He understood the Prime Minister's commitment to King Peter, he acknowledged, and promised to "avoid unnecessary politics and not cause inconvenience to our Allies." If Churchill chose to regard this carefully worded letter as a promise to let Peter return to the throne, that was his gamble. Meanwhile Tito confidently awaited recognition and Allied aid.

"Once Mihailovic is gone," Churchill assured Anthony Eden, "the King's chances will be greatly improved and we can plead his case at Tito's headquarters." He told Eden to reassure their Conservative Party that once Yugoslavia was liberated, all factions would stand aside for an election: "That is a point on which they are all agreed—the King, Tito and the Yugoslav government." In Parliament, Churchill openly praised Tito's Partisans as having had "the honor to be the first to fight the enemy."

American support for Tito was strengthened by important articles in *The New York Times* by publisher Cyrus Sulzberger in December, 1943, revealing Tito as the real hero of Yugoslav national liberation. Tito would have been less than human if he had not been pleased by all this new flattering recognition, even though he knew it reflected Anglo-American strategy to play down his Communism and play up his patriotism, in order to cut the ground from under anti-Communist forces opposed to granting Tito aid and recognition.

Anglo-American supplies began to arrive, first in a trickle, then in huge quantities. Before the war was over, Tito received over 100,000 rifles, 50,000 submachine guns, 600,000 mortars and bombs, 100,000 rounds of ammunition, 260,000 pairs of boots and 175,000 uniforms.

"Now," Tito told Milovan Djilas in delight, "go to Moscow and see how much Grandpapa will bid to match the West!"

Escape
from a Cave

DURING his visit to the Kremlin in February, 1944, Milovan Djilas asked Stalin for a $200,000 loan in addition to arms and equipment. "We will repay the Soviet Union," he assured Stalin, "immediately after Yugoslavia is liberated."

"You insult me!" the Russian dictator scoffed. "The amount you ask is a trifle. As for the weapons, you are shedding your blood, and you expect me to charge you for them? I am not a merchant, Djilas; we are not merchants. You are fighting for the same cause we are. We are duty-bound to share with you whatever we have!"

Stalin's sudden liberality after his long, chronic deafness to Tito's appeals, Djilas knew, was the product of the United States–British decision to drop the Chetniks and support the Partisans. But Stalin was still worried about frightening his Allies. "What do you Partisans want with red stars on your caps?" he complained to Djilas. "By God, stars aren't necessary!" He showed Djilas a map of the world on which the Soviet Union was colored red, making it seem the dominant area on earth. He warned darkly, "They will never accept the idea that so great a space should be red—never, never!"

He gave Djilas a gift for Tito, an ornamental sword. To Djilas it seemed a hint to muffle their revolutionary aims but keep their weapons ready until the war was over, when a new clash between East and West could be expected. Djilas brought home a symbolic gift of his own for Tito, an ivory chess set he purchased in Cairo.

In London, meanwhile, Churchill moved to get rid of Mihailovic. But the Royalist Prime Minister, Bozidar Puric, flatly refused to repudiate Mihailovic or endorse free elections for Yugoslavia. King Peter appealed in vain to his fellow king, Britain's George VI: "I cannot renounce my people, my army, the traditions of my ancestors—I would rather die than do that!" Then he begged Roosevelt to intervene, but the American President only referred him to Churchill: "Please accept his advice as if it was my own."

And Churchill's advice was blunt; it was either Mihailovic's neck or King Peter's. If Puric would not dump Mihailovic, then Puric must be dumped. The King yielded gloomily, and Puric "resigned." He was replaced as Prime Minister by Ivan Subasic, former Governor of Croatia. On June 16, 1944, Subasic signed an agreement with Tito to cooperate in a postwar government free of collaborators.

Mihailovic's doom was finally sealed.

Hitler, however, was not yet finished with the stubborn guerrilla fighter who had upset his military timetable, robbed him of a swift victory in Russia and still pinned down Nazi forces badly needed on the Russian front. He summoned his ace commando, SS *Sturmbannführer* Colonel Otto Skorzeny, who had led the brilliant rescue that had snatched Mussolini from Allied captivity. Hitler's order was brusque:

"Get Tito—dead or alive!"

Skorzeny flew to Belgrade. Where was the Partisan marshal? Conflicting Nazi intelligence reports placed him in five different mountain areas. Disgusted, Skorzeny went on Tito's trail himself. He finally tracked his prey to a cave headquarters in a cliff overlooking the town of Drvar and all its approaches. The cave was reported furnished with Turkish rugs, divans and copperware, its damp walls covered with discarded parachutes from Western supply drops.

Tito was identified as "a lean man, always clean-shaven; blond hair turned mostly gray; using steel-rimmed spectacles for reading; wearing a large diamond ring on the little finger of his left hand; smoking cigarettes in a small pipe holder; dressing in a blue-gray uniform with black boots, shoulder holster with a German revolver, and forage cap with red star insignia." The report said he was always accompanied by two bodyguards, secretary Olga Nincic and a captured German wolfhound called Tiger.

Skorzeny asked the German general in charge of the Drvar region for some Partisan uniforms. His plan: a commando raid by parachute drop directly into Tito's headquarters to kidnap him. But the Nazi general gave Skorzeny a chilly reception. He had no intention of letting any Berlin upstart get the credit for capturing Tito. Stalling Skorzeny, he secretly mounted what the Partisans referred to as the Seventh Enemy Offensive—a German parachute attack on Drvar.

The drone of heavy motors woke Tito at dawn on the morning of May 25, 1944. Rushing to the entrance of the cave, he and Kardelj saw the sky filled with billowing canopies. Some paratroops were already on the ground, shooting their way into the village of Drvar below.

A glider sailed directly toward the cave plateau. At the last moment it nose-dived and crashed into the mountain. But German guns began to flash from the village up toward the cave heights. Tito snatched up a rifle and began returning the fire. A Partisan guard beside him fell, hit.

"Come on!" Kardelj urged, pulling Tito away. "They'll be up here in another minute. You've *got* to leave!"

Marko Rankovic waved them to the rear of the cave, where water had worn an opening through the cave roof from a plateau above. The Partisans climbed up the narrow opening with the aid of a rope. Tito sent Olga, Kardelj and his bodyguards up before him, then fastened a sling and sent the dog Tiger up. Finally he scrambled up the rope himself.

Pulling up the rope, the Partisans fled over the plateau into a pine forest. Making their way to the nearest Partisan unit, they were given mounts and galloped off toward the coast. The Nazi paratroops, bursting into the Drvar cave only moments after their flight, found an empty marshal's uniform Moscow had made for Tito as a gift. Then a rearguard division of Partisans fell upon them, forcing the disgusted Germans to battle their way down the mountain.

Skorzeny was furious. "This is what happens," he icily upbraided the chagrined German general whose full-scale airborne invasion of the Drvar valley had been such a dismal failure, "when you use a sledgehammer for an operation that calls for a fine scalpel!"

In Germany, Heinrich Himmler, chief of the Wehrmacht, was both exasperated and impressed. In a directive to Nazi commanders, he said, "I would like to give another example of steadfastness, that of Marshal Tito. . . . Unfortunately he is our opponent. He really has properly earned his title of Marshal. When we catch him we shall do him in at once. You can be sure of that. He is our enemy, but I wish we had a dozen Titos in Germany, men who were leaders and had such great resolution and good nerves that though they were forever encircled they would never give in.

"The man had nothing, nothing at all . . . always encircled, he found a way out every time. . . . He has the cheek to call a battalion a brigade, and we fall for it right away. A brigade? In heaven's name! The military mind at once imagines a group of 6,000–8,000 men. A thousand vagabonds who have been herded together suddenly become a brigade! . . . He is an uncompromising and steadfast commander."

It was an amazing tribute by an enemy; one that could never, of course, be made publicly. For popular consumption Fascist propaganda turned out such "news" items as this from the *Madrid*, Franco's official mouthpiece:

"Passing through villages and settlements, Tito is committing every posible crime. A captive gives an account of the incredible crimes committed by Tito, who kills for the sake of killing. For this reason Tito is greatly feared in Partisan ranks. Nor do the Partisans, following Tito's example, shrink from murder, robbery and other inhuman deeds. Tito wears a long, utterly unkempt beard," etc., etc.

Every available German division was now pressed into action against the fleeing Marshal and his staff, hoping to trap him between the mountains and the Adriatic Sea.

For some time now, Radio Moscow had been urging him to set up his headquarters on the coastal island of Vis, strongly held by the British and Partisans jointly. But Tito had steadfastly refused to leave the mainland. Now the Kremlin flatly ordered him to rendezvous with a British task force in Dalmatia, who would fly him to Vis. He was too valuable a prize for Hitler to risk any more narrow escapes like Drvar, especially with Skorzeny on his trail.

Reluctant to obey, but programmed to "orders from Moscow" by a lifetime of revolutionary discipline, Tito headed for the rendezvous point. En route he was saddened by the endless sight of houses burned down, grass already growing over the charred ruins. Wherever he rode there were gaunt, sick peasants barely surviving in mud hovels and sheds.

Rebuilding the shattered nation, he realized soberly,

was going to be an agonizing task. Could he be as successful
a leader in peace as he had been in war?

Making contact with the British task force, he was flown
to Vis. Partisan headquarters on the island were in a mountain cave shared with the British. Here Tito worked with
the Royal Air Force coordinating airdrops to Partisan units
on the mainland, and providing them for the first time with
air support in their battles against the enemy.

The Russians, to conciliate Tito for their prolonged failure to help him early in the war, surprised him by flying into
Vis the son of his first marriage. Tito blinked in fascination
at a grown-up Zarko Broz, now a handsome Red Army sergeant. He choked up upon noticing that Zarko had an empty
sleeve; one arm had been lost in the Battle for Moscow.
Father embraced son in wordless emotion, two comrades at
opposite ends of the same world battle.

They were compelled to talk in Russian because Zarko
knew no Yugoslav. Providing him with a Partisan uniform,
Tito ordered that his son be taught at once the Serb-Croat
tongue. The head of the Russian military mission that had
brought Zarko with them to Vis was a little cool toward this
move by Tito to "Yugoslavize" his son. Wasn't it enough for
him that Zarko Broz was a fine Russian citizen and soldier,
proud of his Red Army uniform? Was it also just a coincidence that Comrade Tito had left behind his Russian-made
marshal's uniform in the cave at Drvar, and had had a new
one made in Western-occupied Italy?

On August 14, 1944, Tito flew to Naples for a meeting
with Winston Churchill, taking along Zarko and Olga. Serving as interpreter, Olga so charmed Churchill that he later
sent her a golden locket as a gift. The two war leaders met
for the first time at a villa high on the island of Capri, the
Communist in his new uniform of gold braid and red tabs,
the capitalist in loose white ducks and an open-necked shirt.

Tito was amiable but wary. Even now the British Prime

Minister was trying to crush the Greek Partisan movement
in favor of a conservative Resistance group. Tito listened
impassively as Churchill urged his consent to let King Peter
return to the Yugoslav throne. "After all," Churchill said
persuasively, "democracy flowered in England under a constitutional monarchy. And Yugoslavia's international position
after the war would be much stronger under a king."

"I don't agree," Tito replied coolly. "Don't worry, I
have no intention of introducing the Soviet system into
Yugoslavia after the war. Besides I have already agreed to
hold free elections, and your Subasic will be part of my new
democratic government." He did not tell Churchill that what
he had in mind was not the "Soviet system" but his own
brand of "Tito Socialism." As he explained it to Djilas:

"We are not going to make the mistake of 'democracy
first, Socialism afterward.' It will be Socialism first, democracy afterward—if possible. And *not* the American brand
of democracy, where there are only two political parties—
both alike, and both run by big business!"

At the Capri conference Churchill asked Tito what he
thought ought to be done with Germany after the war. Tito
replied, "It must be split in half, one half occupied by you
and the United States, the other by the Soviet Union. And
the occupation must be permanent. Only a divided Germany
will permit Europe to live at peace. If the Germans are
allowed to reunite, they will start a Third World War!"

He never changed that opinion.

Churchill left their meeting irked that Tito would not
commit himself to King Peter, but hopeful that he would not
Communize Yugoslavia, and might be useful as a neutralized
Balkan bridge between East and West.

Ten days later, without a word to the British, Tito suddenly and secretly flew off to Moscow in a Soviet plane that
Stalin sent to fetch him. The purpose of the flight was to
coordinate Partisan and Red Army movements for the final

liberation of Yugoslavia. The Russian forces were overrunning Rumania and thrusting west toward the Yugoslav border.

This was Tito's second meeting with Stalin—now no longer as a shabby revolutionary underling but as a victorious marshal, future head of a nation. Still awed by the craggy master of world Communism, to whom he had devoted a lifetime of blind obedience and loyalty, Tito nevertheless felt a new dignity in his own status. He sought to negotiate with Stalin on the same equal terms on which he had dealt with the Prime Minister of England.

This arrogance did not sit well with Stalin. Communist leaders of smaller nations were, in the Kremlin view, simply puppets to be used as Moscow saw best. Stalin took a dim view of "Comrade Walter's" new, grandiose, Italian-made uniform. He also resented the glamorous publicity the Partisans had been getting in the Western press. And he had not forgiven the peremptory tone Tito had dared to take in his radioed demands for Russian aid. Dmitrov warned Tito privately, "Walter, Walter, Stalin was terribly angry with you because of your telegrams. He stamped with rage!"

Stalin seethed inwardly, but kept his temper, when Tito agreed to "let" Soviet armored forces help the Partisans clear the Germans out of Yugoslavia, with the "understanding" that the Red Army would withdraw soon after Tito's new government took power. There would be plenty of time, Stalin reflected grimly, to teach this insolent Balkan puppy his place. He would soon learn who called the tune in the world of Communism!

So Stalin remained outwardly unruffled during their talk, even though Molotov was aghast when Tito dared contradict Stalin's opinion several times. *No* one ever did that! Worse, Tito bluntly refused to agree to restoration of the Yugoslav monarchy, despite the fact that Stalin had already promised this concession to Churchill.

"My people would not stand for such treason!" Tito said firmly.

Stalin forced a smile. "You don't have to restore the King forever," he insinuated. "Just take him back temporarily, then slip a knife into his back at a suitable moment!"

But Tito stubbornly insisted that if the British tried to force King Peter's restoration, he would fight.

Returning to Vis, he chose a ceremony decorating the First Dalmatian Shock Brigade on September 12, 1944, to declare: "We have won our own rights which must be respected, for we won them with rivers of blood and mountains of blood!"

Churchill did not learn of the Tito-Stalin meeting until his own visit to Moscow on October 9, when Stalin told him about it. The British Prime Minister was indignant at Tito for having "gone behind my back secretly" to deal with Stalin. Told of Churchill's anger, Tito replied coolly, "Mr. Churchill went to Quebec to see President Roosevelt. I had not heard of this visit until after he returned, and I was not angry." He clearly felt himself entitled to the same independence of action as any leader of the big powers.

Churchill, during his October visit to Moscow, asked Stalin, "How would it do for you to have 90 percent predominance in Rumania, for us to have 90 percent of the say in Greece, and go 50-50 about Yugoslavia?" He even wrote out these blunt formulas on a piece of paper. Stalin signified his assent by blue-penciled check marks.

"At length," Churchill recalled, "I said, 'Might it not be thought rather cynical if it seemed we had disposed of these issues, so fateful to millions of people, in an offhand manner? Let us burn the paper.' 'No, you keep it,' said Stalin." And so Churchill and Stalin agreed to joint control of Yugoslavia after the war, neither taking seriously Tito's plan to establish an independent government.

Stalin knew that, regardless of what Churchill expected,

Tito would see to it that Yugoslavia went Communist. The Russian dictator was confident that he had enough pressure points to apply to make sure that the tough-talking maverick would take his orders from the Red Army.

As Soviet Marshal Tolbukhin's Third Ukrainian Army stormed into Yugoslavia, Tito coordinated the movements of his own troops—now 63 divisions with a total of 800,000 fighting men—with those of the Russians. Their combined forces fought ferocious battles with the enemy as they pushed toward Belgrade, where the Germans had dug in for a last-ditch defense. On October 10, 1944, Tito issued a private order to his First Army Group commander: "It is politically important, and it is also my wish, that our units enter Belgrade *first*." He wanted no quarrel later about the Partisan role in liberating his country.

At Churchill's insistence, King Peter made a bid for Tito's goodwill with a BBC broadcast from London, urging "all Serbs, Croats and Slovenes to unite and join the National Liberation Army under the leadership of Marshal Tito." He condemned all collaboration with those who "misuse the name of the King and the authority of the Crown."

Soviet artillery and air support pounded Belgrade for a week as the Germans fiercely fought street by street, house by house, losing 16,000 killed and 9,000 captured. Thousands of Belgrade civilians took part in the fighting to free the city. Russians and Partisans also lost heavily, but Belgrade fell at last on October 20. Yugoslavia was liberated.

The Partisans led by Tito and the Russians led by Tolbukhin entered the nation's capital together. Tito looked around grimly at the ruins left by Red Army bombs and shells and Nazi dynamite; the cost of victory had been high.

But the uprising he had begun in Belgrade three years earlier had finally been won there. And he had no intention of letting anyone take away the spoils of triumph.

"We warn all those who are speculating, inside or outside the country," he declared as he reviewed a parade of the First Proletarian Corps a week later, "that they are grievously mistaken if they think that the fruits for which an ocean of blood has been shed will now slip from our grasp. We will never yield those fruits to anyone!"

Then he raised his voice as though to be heard in the Kremlin and 10 Downing Street: "We are no longer going to be the small change for negotiating deals. In this struggle we have won the right to be treated as equals by the Allies!"

One conflict had ended; a new one had begun.

Black Sheep
from Red Russia

AFTER three long years of daily peril and suffering, misery
and hunger, discomfort and death, Tito did not hesitate to
reward himself with the traditional spoils of victory. No one
enjoyed luxury more than the peasant boy of the Zagorje
who had grown up hungry, sleeping on the floor; who had
been astonished by his first view of upper-class life as a
fourteen-year-old bus boy in a Sisak café; who had spent
over thirty hand-to-mouth years as a hunted revolutionary.

Besides, he told Olga indignantly, the Russian officers
in Belgrade were moving into the best houses they could
find in the fashionable suburbs. Did he, Marshal of Yugoslavia, deserve less than Russian officers and advisers?

Wealthy owners of Belgrade villas, many of them German collaborators, had fled in panic before the city fell to
the liberators. The few who hadn't were either moved un-
ceremoniously into their own servants' quarters, or arrested
on the *prima facie* evidence that they *had* to be collaborators
to have been left in undisturbed possession of their wealth.

Tito and Olga, with Tiger and a staff of voluntary ser-

vants, took over a suburban walled villa. Prince Paul's former White Palace was used for state receptions. Tito took
down Palace portraits of the royal family, replacing them
with pictures of Lenin and Stalin. Olga unstitched royal
monograms from the Palace bed linen.

Belgrade's best tailor was soon busy creating a whole
new wardrobe of flamboyant suits and uniforms for Tito;
fine shirts came from the capital's most fashionable shirt-
maker. Olga saw to it that he was served with the finest
wines in large gold goblets; the best Turkish coffee; the
tastiest *culbastija* and other grilled meats. Tito also acquired
a stable of thoroughbred horses, a speedboat, a yacht and a
fleet of expensive automobiles. *This* was the life. No wonder
King Peter was so anxious to get back on the Yugoslav
throne!

Luxury delighted but did not spoil him. He never forgot
his humble origins or the people who had helped him in his
threadbare days. When a letter of congratulations came from
Franjo Podupski, the cabinet-maker who had made free
coffins for his two infants who had died in Veliko Trojstvo,
Tito invited him to his villa as a guest and showered him
with gifts. Tito also welcomed his aunt Ana who arrived in
Belgrade "to see my nephew." When he showed her his
beautiful horses in the Guard Stable, she sighed, "Nothing
like them in Kumrovec!"

Except for putting on weight, he remained unchanged
—friendly, informal, tolerant, fond of jokes. Once at a dinner
in his honor at the American Embassy, the phone rang near
him. Answering it himself, he pretended to be the Ambassador's butler. "Don't you know better," he roared into the
phone in mock anger, "than to disturb the American Ambassador when he is entertaining the *great* Marshal Tito?"

But if he enjoyed the affluent life without losing his
sense of humor, secret notions of grandeur were suggested

by his favorite bronze decorating his villa—a bust of Napoleon. This fact did not go unreported to Joseph Stalin.

Always the realist, the sardonic observer in the Kremlin was satisfied with the power situation in the Balkans. The Western Allies had no troops of their own there except a small British force in Greece. Nothing could balk Stalin's plans for eastern Europe as long as Yugoslavia was safely under Communist control. And for that he relied far less on the unpredictable Tito than the Third Ukrainian Army.

He was merely amused, at first, at complaints by Russian commanders in Belgrade that Tito and his staff were acting "as if they, and not the Red Army, had liberated Yugoslavia." But he was outraged when Milovan Djilas dared to complain of the "unworthy behavior" of Russian officers who were "destroying the reputation of the Red Army by immoral conduct." Such behavior, Djilas insisted, contrasted shamefully with that of the British Military Mission.

On December 30, 1944, Tito had issued an order for all Partisans to "follow the example of the Red Army where the strictest discipline prevails side by side with the spirit of comradeship." But to the chagrin and astonishment of the Partisan leaders, who had always dealt severely with petty looting and crime in their own ranks, Red Army officers in Belgrade let their troops loot, rape and run wild.

How was it possible, Djilas protested, that the imperialistic British in Yugoslavia were behaving so decently, while comrades from Moscow were outraging Partisan hospitality? Shocked, he cited 111 cases of Red Army rape and murder, and 1,204 incidents of looting with assault.

Stalin was infuriated. After hours of brooding he wired Tito: "I understand the difficulty of your situation after the liberation of Belgrade, but I am surprised that a few incidents and offenses committed by individual officers and soldiers are being generalized and extended to the whole of

the Red Army. You should not so offend an army which is
helping you to get rid of the Germans. Is it so difficult to
understand that there are black sheep in every family? The
soldiers of the Red Army cry out in pain at such an undeserved insult!"

Boiling with anger, he roared at Yugoslav representatives in Moscow, "Does Djilas, who is himself a writer, not
know what human suffering and the human heart are? Can't
he understand it if a soldier who has crossed thousands of
kilometers through blood and fire and death has fun with a
woman or takes some trifle?"

The real cause of Stalin's fury was the presumption of
Tito and the "impudent" Djilas in challenging the right of
the Red Army to behave as it pleased in a Communist country.

King Peter, also provoked with Tito for anti-Royalist
remarks, repudiated the Subasic-Tito agreement his own
minister had signed. Exasperated, Churchill agreed with
Roosevelt and Stalin at the Yalta Conference that the treaty
should be endorsed anyhow, regardless of King Peter. Stalin
was delighted, feeling that this Big Three decision had put
Yugoslavia in his pocket. He was soon to be disillusioned.

On March 7, 1945, Tito set up a provisional government
of Democratic Federal Yugoslavia, with himself as Prime
Minister and Subasic as Foreign Minister. Subasic quickly
discovered, however, that all real power had been allocated
to his "assistant," Edvard Kardelj. Tito divided the country
into six "people's republics"—Serbia, Croatia, Slovenia,
Bosnia-Herzegovina, Macedonia and Montenegro.

He also demanded that the Allies permit him to annex
the port city of Trieste, which the Partisans had captured
from the Italians, along with an adjoining 3,000-square-mile
province, Venezia Giulia, with its largely Slovene population.
Worried, the Allied command rushed British and American
troops to prevent annexation of this territory.

Tito ordered his commanders on May 3, 1945, "Retain the towns at all costs. Beware of provocations, but stand firm." He was indignant at the Western move to hold the area for Italy. Italy—Hitler's Axis partner until she had been knocked out of the war! "Churchill and Roosevelt are afraid if they let us have Trieste," Tito told Kardelj, "the Italians will get mad at them and vote Communist in spite!"

Partisans and local sympathizers plastered Trieste with fiery banners: DEATH TO FASCISM, LIBERTY TO THE PEOPLE! . . . TITO IS OURS AND WE ARE TITO'S! . . . TRIESTE IS SLOVENIAN!

The British commander in Trieste, Field Marshal Harold Alexander, testily protested to Tito that the behavior of the Partisans was "all too reminiscent of Hitler, Mussolini and Japan," and that the Allies had just fought a war to stop the forceful seizure of territory. Bitter clashes broke out between Anglo-American and Partisan forces.

On May 6, four British pursuit planes strafed Fourth Army troops in the Yugoslav occupation zone. Stalin felt compelled to come to Tito's defense in this flagrant attack on a Communist ally. He darkly warned the West against using force to drive the Yugoslavs out of Trieste. President Truman, the new occupant in the White House, later admitted that the situation was growing so tense he feared the outbreak of war between East and West. He and Churchill argued with Stalin against Tito's claim of the Trieste area.

"It would be an undeserved insult," Stalin replied, "to refuse Yugoslavia the right to occupy the territory retaken from the enemy after the Yugoslav people have made so many sacrifices . . . for the common cause of the United Nations." He used the word "retaken" because Trieste had been part of the Austro-Hungarian Empire until World War I, when it had been awarded to Italy as war spoils.

Stalin could hardly fail to support Tito's right to annex territory without laying open to question his own postwar spoils in eastern Europe. But at the same time he privately ordered Tito to be cautious and not provoke the Anglo-American bloc too far. Tito's reply came on May 27, 1945, while visiting Slovenia, in an indignant speech that carried a sting for Moscow as well as London and Washington.

"It is said that this war is a just war, and we have considered it as just," he declared. "However, we also seek a just end. We demand that everyone shall be master in his own house. We do not want to pay for others; we do not want to be used as a bribe in international bargaining. We do not want to become involved in any policy primarily concerned with spheres of influence!"

Shocked, Stalin fired off an angry wire to Kardelj in Belgrade, charging that Tito's speech was "an unfriendly attack on the Soviet Union." Any more outbursts like that from Tito, Stalin warned grimly, and Moscow would be "forced to reply with open criticism in the press and disavow him!"

Alarmed at this threat of Kremlin excommunication, Kardelj hastily agreed with the Russian Ambassador in Belgrade that Tito had indeed gone too far, and expressed appreciation for Moscow's "well-timed criticism."

"Kardelj said," reported Ambassador I. V. Sadchikov to Stalin, "he would like the Soviet Union to regard them, not as representatives of another country, capable of solving questions independently, but as representatives of one of the future Soviet Republics . . . that is, that our relations should be based on the prospect of Yugoslavia becoming in the future a constituent part of the USSR."

This humble-pie reply mollified Stalin, who began to muse about getting rid of Tito and replacing him with Kardelj. To teach Tito a lesson, Stalin passed the word quietly to Truman and Churchill that he was really not too interested in the Trieste question, in effect reassuring them they could feel free to take a tough line with Tito over it.

Stalin had a second motive. He didn't have to worry about the Yugoslavs; they were safely locked into the Communist world. But by allowing Italy's claim to Trieste, he could strengthen the hand of Italian Communists and help them win seats in their coming elections. So at a London meeting of the Council of Foreign Ministers, Molotov remarked for the Italian press, "Only those territories belonging to the Croats and Slovenes should be turned over to Yugoslavia. As for the territories that are Italian in character, it is proper for Italy to have them."

Washington and London maintained their bid for the Italian vote by standing firm against Tito and also letting the Italians know it. "The entire orientation of the Italian government," President Eisenhower later wrote, "depended to a large extent on the outcome of the Trieste negotiations." At last Tito grudgingly agreed to a temporary compromise that divided the disputed Trieste territory into two zones of occupation, one Allied, one Partisan.

Tito felt bitter that Moscow had seen fit to use Yugoslavia as a pawn in a power struggle with the West. He still felt committed to the Communism of Stalin—but was that really the same as the *Russianism* of Stalin? The notion bemused him. Could it be possible to build a Communism tailored to the specific needs of Yugoslavia, but not necessarily to the needs of the Soviet Union? Did Stalin, in other words, own the copyright on Communism?

Although Hitler's Germany surrendered on May 8, 1945, the fierce resistance of the Nazi armies in Yugoslavia dragged on for another week. So even as the whole free world was celebrating victory in Europe, the Partisans continued fighting until General von Lohr, who had come so close to destroying them in seven offensives, finally capitulated on May 15. But it was a bitter triumph for Yugoslavs.

Their nation lay devastated, exhausted. Almost two million people had been killed—one in eight—and perhaps twice as many wounded. Entire towns and villages had been ravaged. Half the nation's homes and livestock had been destroyed; a third of its industry ruined; half its coal mines flooded; half its railroad tracks torn up; most of its rolling stock confiscated by Germany. Without outside help, Tito knew, recovery from the war would take generations.

He was grateful when large-scale aid began to arrive from UNRRA, the UN fund to which the United States was the largest single contributor. "Your assistance," he told Fund Director Fiorello LaGuardia, ex-Mayor of New York City, "will relieve want in devastated areas threatened by famine."

Touring the country with Tito to inspect war damage, LaGuardia was impressed by the tough courage and independence of the Yugoslavs he met. "It's easy to be a Tito," he grinned, "in a country with men like these!" Tito warmed to LaGuardia's sense of humor and lack of pretension. "He was not only a humanitarian," the Marshal said afterward, "but also a genuine democrat."

Estimating the damage suffered by Yugoslavia at the hands of the Germans and Italians at $61 billion, Tito demanded that the Allies compensate his country by turning over to it complete German factories. As for Italy, he declared, "Those tens of thousands of men, women and children butchered and shot by the Italian Fascists in Slovenia, Dalmatia, Montenegro, Herzegovina and elsewhere can never be compensated, but the burned-down villages and razed cities and everything looted must be made good at the expense of the reactionaries; and the Italian people should see to it."

He held the first general elections of postwar Yugoslavia on November 11, 1945. Voters were offered a Marxist-style choice of 510 candidates—470 Communist Party members and 40 nonmembers who had Party approval. The polling places were vigorously patrolled by YCP soldiers and civilians.

It was no great surprise, therefore, when the newly elected constituent assembly voted unanimously to abolish the monarchy and declare Yugoslavia a "Federal People's Republic." Tito was made President, his personal dictatorship assured by tight control of government and Party machinery, armed forces, foreign office and the economy. He held no less than seven different key posts and titles.

London and Washington were dismayed at this interpretation of his promise to hold free elections. A United States State Department official told the press, "In view of conditions existing in Yugoslavia, it cannot be said that those guarantees of freedom have been honored, nor that the elections conducted on November 11 provided opportunity for a free choice of the people's representatives."

Nevertheless, faced with Tito's *fait accompli*, Washington glumly recognized the new regime, hopeful that "in the evolution of events Yugoslavia would develop conditions of which the United States would fully and wholeheartedly approve." Tito shrugged off this slap on the wrist. He had Western recognition; that was all that mattered.

He did not really feel morally obligated by the wartime treaty he had signed with Subasic. "We *had* to accept this agreement," he explained, "because the Western powers stubbornly insisted on it." He told a correspondent of the French Communist paper, *Humanité*, "The old politicians emigrated while the people were fighting for freedom."

Subasic bitterly resigned his titular post as Foreign Minister right after the elections. There was no further point in a Royalist minister trying to stay on in a Communist dictatorship that had kicked the monarchy out. Tito shed no tears. Edvard Kardelj, the mustached, spectacled, lame ex-teacher and Spanish War veteran, was immediately named the new

Foreign Minister. Other key cabinet posts also went to the Partisan comrades who had fought beside Tito.

Milovan Djilas, the huge Montenegro firebrand who had once peddled milk door-to-door to pay for his law education, was put in charge of press and radio. Alexander "Marko" Rankovic, the tough, squat ex-village tailor, became Minister of Police. Black Zujovic, the Serb military strategist, became Minister of Finance. Andrija Hebrang, the Partisan sadistically tortured by the Ustase, became Minister of Industry. Tito also found a place for his old Marxist tutor and fellow jailbird, Mosa Pijade, who became Vice President of Serbia on the Federal Executive Council.

Tito's first new laws were intended to strengthen the pride and security of each Yugoslav nationality, at the same time they promoted national unity. It was made a crime to provoke hatred or discriminate against any Yugoslav minority. Each republic was allowed to use its own mother tongue as its official language. Wherever possible, national minorities were to have their own schools, papers, broadcasts.

At the same time students were encouraged to attend universities outside their own republics; workers to vacation and take jobs in other republics. One young teacher in Celije said, "Tito has made me a Yugoslav first, a Slovene second, a Communist third—and proud of being all three!"

As Chief of the Secret Police, the UDBA, Rankovic lost little time in arranging the trials of the Partisans' enemies. "Who is against Socialism is an enemy," he declared, "and must be made harmless." Reprisals were swift and sure against both anti-Partisans of the war period and those who persisted in opposition afterward. Cries of persecution and "purge" were raised abroad. There is little doubt that there were some unfair trials and hasty executions.

Most prisoners tried, however, were Nazi collaborators, Ustase terrorists and similar unsavory characters. Typical was Svetozar Vujkovic, an old police agent who had com-

manded a concentration camp at Banjica, where tens of thousands of Serbs, Moslems and Jews alike were murdered. "I was merely obeying orders as an employee of the state," Vujkovic whimpered at the trial. "I killed no one personally."

He was sentenced to death and shot.

One UDBA agent arrested Madame Fidlerica, the café owner of Lepoglava who had once helped Tito smuggle forbidden books into prison. Notified, Tito reacted sharply.

"She used to help us simply because she was a good Christian," he told Rankovic. "Now she is helping the reactionaries for the same reason. She sees no difference at all and believes she is doing a good thing. Let the old woman alone!" Madame Fidlerica was promptly released.

The most celebrated Yugoslav prisoner to stand trial was Draza Mihailovic, who had been captured hiding in a foxhole in a forest. When he was brought into court in a uniform stripped of all insignia, the crowd booed, jeered and hissed, with loud cries of "Hang him!" He faced his accusers with quiet dignity, knowing that his own son Branko, a Partisan, had denounced his "treacherous work."

~~~~~~~~~~~~~~~~~~~~~~~~~~~~**11**

"Nobody Is Going to Buy Tito!"

YUGOSLAV Royalists in London charged that Branko Mihailovic had been forced to accuse his father to escape torture at the hands of Rankovic's UDBA. But Churchill admitted, "Mihailovic . . . commanders made accommodations with the German and Italian troops to be left alone in certain mountain areas in return for doing little or nothing against the enemy."

It was the kindest possible *apologia pro vita sua* for a collaborationist. In contrast, Churchill noted admiringly of Tito's Partisans: "No reprisals, however bloody, upon hostages or villages deterred them. For them it was death or freedom." Now that they had won, it was freedom for them and death for Mihailovic, who was found guilty and shot.

To keep a tight grip on their new power, Tito gave a free hand to Rankovic's political police. Imitating Stalin's Cheka, they indexed the nation's workers with loyalty ratings ranging from "trustworthy" to "dangerous." Communist Party membership—475,000 by 1950—was limited to those

124

with top ratings. Only they, too, were eligible for appointment or election to important government jobs.

Washington received conflicting reports as to the degree of freedom allowed by the Tito regime. One State Department observer in Belgrade found a genuine desire to provide "freedom for all people," as well as an attitude "extremely friendly to the United States." On the other hand, Major Temple Fielding, serving with a United States military mission to Belgrade, deplored the death penalty for criticizing Tito or the Soviet Union, and took a caustic view of UNRRA food distribution: "If you are a Partisan, you eat; if you are not, you starve."

Tito became increasingly irked by large amounts of American aid being given to West Germany, while the United States continued to oppose Yugoslav claims in Trieste. He expressed his pique by protesting constant "violation of Yugoslavia's air space" by United States planes flying between Austria and Italy. His protests were not taken seriously.

On August 9, 1946, an unarmed American C-47 was fired on by Yugoslav fighter planes and forced down near Lyublyana; its nine passengers were arrested. Ten days later a second C-47 was shot down in flames inside the Yugoslav border, with five of the crew killed. Outraged, the US State Department called upon Tito to release the surviving American prisoners and pay half a million dollars in damages, or face charges in the UN. Tito released the airmen; tempers cooled on both sides, and the matter was settled diplomatically.

But when the United States Ambassador, Richard C. Patterson, called on Tito, he was told, "You expect me to be grateful for the American aid I get through UNRRA, but you refuse to help us build the new industries we need. You even warn that the aid we get will be cut off unless we 'behave ourselves'—meaning, I assume, doing as Washington tells us."

"That is not our intention, Mr. Marshal—"

"But you give *more* aid and goodwill to a defeated Germany—the common enemy who invaded Yugoslavia—than to us, their victims! Nobody is going to buy Tito, Mr. Ambassador. If there are strings to your dollars, keep them!"

"You will never inspire goodwill," Patterson reproached him coldly, "by shooting down our airplanes."

"Nor you," Tito growled, "by violating our sovereignty!"

He also angered opinion in the United States by his attacks on religion. His anticlericalism stemmed less from his personal or Marxist atheism than from his nationalistic objection to a rival source of power, especially to churches controlled from outside the country. With Yugoslav and Italian interests in conflict over Trieste, for example, he resented Vatican influence on Yugoslav Catholics.

"That authority has always been more in sympathy with Italy than with our nation," he bluntly told a delegation of Catholic clergy on June 5, 1945. "I would like to see the Catholic Church in Croatia enjoy more independence."

His antagonism toward the Vatican also had its roots in the war. He blamed the Pope for supporting the Ustase because they were Croat Catholics, and also for helping Hitler's Ustase puppet, Dr. Pavelic, escape to Argentina.

The Vatican, in turn, denounced Tito for executing priests as collaborators during the first two years of his regime, and confiscating over 160,000 acres of Church lands in Croatia, Serbia and Slovenia. The Vatican was particularly bitter about the trial in 1946 of the Primate of Yugoslavia, Archbishop Aloysius Stepinac, as an "enemy of the people."

Stepinac was charged with publicly blessing the Nazi Army, as shown in captured newsreels; sitting in Pavelic's Parliament despite the Ustase atrocities against Serbs, Jews and Partisans; forcing prisoners to choose between conversion and death by Ustase; and leading Yugoslavia's priesthood in postwar opposition to government measures against the Vatican.

Stepinac steadfastly denied that he had committed anything that could be called a crime, because the new government's laws had not existed during the war. He bitterly attacked the "national liberation movement" for having killed 260 to 270 priests. "In no civilized state in the world," he cried, "would so many priests be punished for such crimes as have been imputed to them. . . . In no other civilized state would death have been meted out; only, at most, a prison sentence. You have made a fatal mistake in murdering priests. The people will not forgive you for that."

Whatever collaboration he had given the Nazis or Ustase, Stepinac insisted, had been unavoidable and for the purpose of easing their harsh acts against the populace. The evidence suggested that while he had been pro-Fascist and a collaborationist, he had become sickened by Pavelic's atrocities and had made some effort to protect Ustase victims.

"You will be condemning an innocent man," he told the court defiantly. But he was sentenced to sixteen years at hard labor, plus confiscation of all his property. There was an indignant protest from the Vatican.

"We certainly cannot allow anyone from the Vatican to interfere in our internal affairs," Tito replied sharply. But in November, 1950, chiefly as a concession to American Catholic opinion, he publicly offered to free Stepinac if the Archbishop would retire to a monastery or leave the country. Stepinac coldly refused. A year later Tito released him anyhow, confining him to his native village near Zagreb. When Rome promptly made him a cardinal, Tito testily severed relations with the Vatican. The stormy Stepinac affair came to an end with his death in 1960.

Tito was also intent upon breaking the power and

wealth of the Serbian Orthodox Church, which vehemently
opposed Communism. The Orthodox hierachy demanded
establishment as the state religion; compulsory religious
education; army chaplains; and denial of aid to any atheistic
organization.

The Communist Party sent a crowd of supporters under
the windows of Metropolitan Josip, Acting Head of the
Serb Orthodox Church, to shout, "Death to Josip!" Appear-
ing on a balcony above them, the Metropolitan demanded
ironically, "Which of your leaders are you shouting against—
Josip Broz or Josip Stalin?" He was later sent to prison for
three years for "criticizing the religious situation in Russia."

During its land reform program the government
stripped the rich Serb Orthodox Church of 90 percent of
the lands it owned. Tito also confiscated its foundations and
trust funds, and turned some of its elaborate churches and
monasteries into public museums, workers' vacation resorts
and hospitals.

Gradually, however, Tito began to substitute persuasion
for intimidation, and Moslem, Protestant and Jewish leaders
began making their peace with the Communist government.

Some American church leaders, accusing Tito of religious persecution, demanded that the United States cease
all aid to Yugoslavia. Tito promptly invited a group of
American religious leaders to visit his country and judge for
themselves. He promised complete freedom of movement
and investigation.

A commission of seven liberal Protestant churchmen
accepted, and spent two weeks traveling around Yugoslavia.
They found churches of all denominations full of worshippers
on Sundays, and held conferences with Catholic, Orthodox,
Moslem, Jewish and Protestant religious leaders. Allowed a
private interview in prison with Archbishop Stepinac, they
decided that he had been properly convicted, and was

guilty of all the charges the government had made against him.

They concluded that Americans had been getting a distorted picture of Tito's Yugoslavia. "We have been deeply impressed by the fact," they reported, "that in spite of the behavior of certain church leaders and individual priests, there exists extensive tolerance toward religion, or rather toward the churches, in Yugoslavia."

Nevertheless, Tito saw his country's different churches and religious credos as divisive, pulling Yugoslavs apart into hostile factions. In contrast, he tried to make Communist doctrine cohesive, binding all groups.

"My greatest satisfaction," he told a visiting British MP in November, 1945, "is when I see the unanimity of the people in their efforts to build the country, when I see that we were able to unite all the nationalities and prevent fratricidal strife."

Having disposed of his principal enemies—the Germans, the Italians, the Ustase, King Peter, Subasic, Mihailovic, Stepinac—Tito turned all his energies to rearranging the social structure of his shattered country.

He first passed the Agrarian Reform Law of August 23, 1945, liquidating all big estates and limiting peasant holdings of farmlands to thirty-eight acres, on Lenin's theory that "the land belongs to those who cultivate it." The law also confiscated land belonging to banks, corporations, monasteries and absentee landlords. About 80 percent of confiscated land was distributed to poor and landless peasants and to war veterans. The rest went into collective farms.

To step up and control the nation's food supply, Tito tried to force many peasants into Soviet-type *kolkhozes* as Stalin had done. Years later a peasant named Mijo Stefanovic recalled, "After the war the Communists confiscated 120 of my sheep, 130 of my pigs, all my machinery, and threw me in jail for a year and a half because I refused to join the local cooperative farm." But strong peasant opposition finally decided Tito to go slow on collectivization, and dissatisfied peasants were allowed to quit the cooperatives.

On January 31, 1946, he gave Yugaslovia a new constitution, modeled after the Soviet Union's. By the end of the year he had nationalized industry and commerce, and in November launched his first Five-Year Plan to turn Yugoslavia from a backward agricultural country into a modern industrial nation. To help his people make this transition, he launched a campaign to wipe out illiteracy.

On a trip through postwar Yugoslavia, American journalist Ella Winter described seeing "illiterate peasants sitting on the ground in a circle learning to spell, their first word being *Ti-to, Ti-to.*"

Stalin was deeply annoyed by Tito's decision to industrialize, and did everything he could to keep Yugoslavia a Russian colony for raw materials. "What do you want with a heavy industry?" he scoffed at Tito. "We have everything you need in the Urals!" But in July, 1948, Tito told the 5th YCP Congress what he had told Stalin:

"We did not wish to halt halfway: to depose the King and abolish the monarchy, and to come to power only to share it with representatives of the capitalist class, who would continue to exploit the working masses of Yugoslavia." No, Yugoslavia had to make basic changes in its economy— take it over, control it, change it, expand it.

More and more Tito was beginning to realize that the interests of a Communist Yugoslavia were *not* the same as those of a Communist Russia. Didn't he have the same obligation, he asked Djilas, to think first of his own people, as Stalin obviously did of the Russian people? Stalin expected him to recognize Soviet needs, but had Stalin cooperated with Tito's demand for Trieste? No, because he was more interested in wooing the Italian Communists.

An Italian peace treaty on February 10, 1947, created a Free Territory of Trieste, with a promise to return it later to Italy. Yugoslavia received only Venezia Giulia. The Italians credited the United States with thwarting Tito, and elected Social Democrats to office in the 1948 elections. Stalin's maneuvers not only failed to help the Italian Communists but also embittered the Communists of Yugoslavia.

Tito decided that his country's postwar poverty demanded drastic economic solutions, no matter whether they pleased Stalin or not. Even by 1950 the average Yugoslav still had to work five weeks to earn enough to buy a pair of shoes. "Think of your hometown," he explained to an American correspondent, "if in every eighth home, either a mother, father or child had been killed. Then you'll understand our problems!"

Tito's decision to go his own way economically, independent of Stalin's wishes, was reached only after anguished soul-searching. His lifelong allegiance to the Kremlin was as firmly ingrained as the devotion of world Catholics to the Vatican. If they considered the dogma of the Pope infallible, Communists had absolute faith that Stalin's judgments and orders were faultless. The Kremlin no more expected defiance from any nation's Communist Party than the Vatican did from any nation's Catholic Church.

In fact, the Russian ambassador in Belgrade made it clear to Tito that to erase Milovan Djilas' "slur" on the Red Army, the Yugoslav press, radio and theatre must glorify the role of the Red Army as the country's liberators.

When Tito, accompanied by Djilas, went to Moscow in the spring of 1945 to sign a mutual assistance treaty, they found Stalin in a cool mood. He still had not forgiven Djilas for daring to "slander" Red Army behavior. To put the Yugoslavs in their place, Stalin sneered at the Partisans, comparing them unfavorably to the Bulgarian Army.

Stung, Tito flushed. He was no mere puppet set up by

the Red Army; he and the Partisans had fought their own battles for almost four years without so much as a bullet's help from the Russians. As one Partisan had proudly told an American reporter in shaky English, "When Tito said rise up—we rised!" Now Tito snapped, "If our army has any weaknesses, we will quickly correct them."

At a drinking party in the Kremlin, Stalin proposed a toast to the Yugoslav Army, but added cynically, "May it yet learn to fight well on level ground!" As the toasts grew more copious and the celebrants more wobbly, Stalin began to hum and dance by himself. "How strong you are, Tova-rich!" Molotov called out sycophantically. Stalin suddenly stopped and grew tipsily moody. "Oh, no, no," he sighed. "I won't live long. The physiological laws are having their way." He pretended a delight that Tito was younger, and would be spared to lead Europe one day. Then with a sly smile he slipped his hands under Tito's armpits and jovially lifted the tough Yugoslav leader off the floor three times in time to a Russian folk melody on the gramophone.

"But there is *still* strength in me!" he chuckled ominously. Unfazed, Tito dropped a subtle warning of his own.

"No matter how much any of us may love the Father-land of Socialism, the USSR," he told Stalin at one point, "he can in no way love his own country—which is *also* build-ing Socialism—the less!" The Soviet leader gave no sign that he recognized this test shot across Moscow's bow.

"Yes," he nodded urbanely. "Today Socialism is possible even under the English monarchy. Revolution is no longer necessary everywhere. Just recently a delegation of British Laborites was here, and we talked about this."

But that was not the same as agreeing that there could be a separate road to Socialism for a country *already* ruled by Communist ideology. In Stalin's eyes that automatically made it a Russian province. After the party Tito growled irritably to Djilas, "I don't know what the devil is wrong with these Russians that they drink so much. Plain decadence!"

When they returned to Yugoslavia, Tito's mind was firmly made up. Hadn't Lenin himself pointed the way for other Communist countries to develop, when he defined Communism as "the Soviet Republic—plus electrification"? If industrialization had worked wonders for the Russians, then why not for the Yugoslavs? In an interview with Ella Winter, Tito indicated he felt his country was being exploited:

"They take our bauxite, all our raw materials, and our countrymen have to emigrate, a million and a half of them, because there's not enough left to make a livelihood here. We should *keep* our raw materials, and make it possible for our countrymen to live in their own homeland!"

Ironically, the revolutionist who had once considered his only loyalty international, now had become a patriotic Yugoslav nationalist under the pressure of responsibility.

Increasing signs of his political independence did not go unnoticed by the Kremlin. Speaking at Zagreb in November, 1946, Tito hailed Yugoslavia's peasants as the strongest pillar of his Communist state. This was a flat contradiction of the Marx-Lenin-Stalin dictum that the working classes, not the peasantry, were the backbone of Socialism.

Seeking to unify and control the new Communist regimes the Red Army had brought to power in East Europe, Stalin organized a new Cominform international—a postwar version of the Comintern he had disbanded during the war. He gave grudging consent to Dmitrov's plan for a Balkans defense pact. When Tito went to Poland, Czechoslovakia, Albania and Hungary to sign mutual assistance treaties, enthusiastic crowds turned out everywhere to give him a thundering ovation.

Stalin was stunned when Tito, without first consulting the Kremlin, proposed a new Yugoslav-Bulgarian Federation, with the possibility of Poland, Czechoslovakia and Rumania joining later. Then Tito made a speech criticizing the Communist Parties of other Cominform countries for their failings, as though he, not Stalin, were the arbiter of Marxist orthodoxy. Now Stalin lost his temper.

Was Tito daring to bid for the leadership of the Balkans, setting himself up as a rival to the *Vozhd* in the Kremlin? A Balkan Federation—*without* the Soviet Union? The little Marshal from Belgrade was obviously getting too big for his britches and would have to be taught a lesson!

Stalin had destroyed far more powerful Communist leaders than Tito who had dared assert their independence of him. But this was not the strategic time to demolish the Yugoslav upstart. Stalin had his hands full with a burgeoning Cold War against the West, and could not at the moment afford a split in his ranks. Tito was still, at least, offering lip service of loyalty to the Kremlin.

Behind the mask of a bland smile, Stalin could patiently hoard grudges for years. "There's nothing sweeter than to bide the proper moment for revenge," he once explained, "to insert the knife, twist it, and then go home for a good night's sleep." The time of the knife would come.

Yes, Tito could be sure of that. *It would come!*

~~~~~~12

David
Versus Goliath

SOVIET Foreign Minister Molotov sent a sharp note of protest against Tito's treatment of Ambassador Sadchikov.

"What is he complaining of?" Tito replied. "He is shown
exactly the same courtesies and consideration we show to the
ambassadors of every other nation."

"*That* is what he is complaining of," Molotov pointed
out coldly. "In a truly Communist nation, the Russian Ambassador is certainly entitled to expect a special status above
that of ordinary diplomats from bourgeois governments!"

There was more in this exchange than met the eye.
Molotov correctly suspected that Tito, by the equal treatment of Sadchikov with Western ambassadors, was signaling
to Moscow, London and Washington his political independence. The Soviet Foreign Office was equally unhappy about
a conversation with Tito reported by Soviet Marshal Tolbukhin, who had discovered that they had fought each other
on the Carpathian front in 1915, when Tolbukhin had been
a Russian noncom.

"You shot at us," he reproached Tito half-jokingly.

135

Tito had shrugged. "You shot at us."

"But you shot at *us*. At Russians!"

"Well, you were the soldiers of the Russian Tsar, and we were the soldiers of the Austrian Tsar!"

Stalin decided to begin applying pressure. Black Zujovic and Andrija Hebrang were the two members of Tito's cabinet considered fanatically loyal to Moscow. He ordered them to block Tito's program for industrialization. They dutifully began to undermine it on the Central Committee while Tito was traveling in Prague and Warsaw.

Informed of this upon his return, Tito was deeply hurt and troubled. He had a personal affection for both men stemming from their valiant fight beside him as Partisans, especially Black Zujovic. But he felt that he had to choose between them and his Five-Year Plan. Zujovic was severely reprimanded, and Hebrang was fired.

Long hours of conscientious work did not stunt Tito's love of the affluent life. His dozen elegant uniforms were strained by hearty eating and drinking, often requiring him to diet between banquets. He loved parties which let him waltz with the ladies and sometimes dance a peasant *kolo*. He also enjoyed chess or billiards with skilled opponents.

His closest friends were cabinet members Djilas, Rankovic and Kardelj, who occupied the luxurious villas surrounding his own. Olga had vanished, her place taken by a new secretary, Colonel Branko Vatzinic. Tito was by this time divorced from Herta. Their son Misko occasionally visited him from Slovenia. Tito also saw Zarko now and then; but for the most part he lived as a carefree bachelor.

He and the other Yugoslav leaders were offended by the wild parties thrown by Red Army officers who occupied villas around them in the suburb of Dedinye. They winced every night at the bedlam of smashing glasses, breaking furniture, wild orgies and exploding weapons. A favorite

Russian party game was called "Cuckoo." The lights would be turned out; all would hide; someone would shout "Cuckoo!"; guns would be fired in his direction. The game ended when a Cuckoo-caller was either wounded or killed. Tito grimly determined to get rid of his Russian neighbors at the first opportunity.

No fool, he was suspicious of an invitation to Moscow on March 1, 1948, to "discuss the complications that have set in between Yugoslavia and the Soviet Union." Tito pleaded illness and let Kardelj go in his place. Both knew that Stalin would not spring a trap for a mere Foreign Minister.

Stalin stormed at Kardelj for Yugoslavia's "insubordination" in planning a Balkan Federation without first consulting with the Soviet Union. "You do not consult with us on any question!" Stalin fumed. "There will be no such Federation! Not only that, but Tito must stop helping Greek Partisans against the British. All he is doing is inflaming the West against us, as though *we* are responsible!"

Tito made no direct reply. Instead he cooly informed the Russian Ambassador in Belgrade that Yugoslavia could no longer afford to pay for so large a staff of Soviet "advisers," whose salaries were four times higher than that of any Yugoslav minister. He also rejected a Moscow demand that Rankovic's secret police be put under Soviet control.

"We regard it as improper," Tito snapped, "for the agents of the Soviet Intelligence . . . to recruit our citizens for *their* service!" Stalin was flabbergasted. He roared an order for the return of all Soviet military advisers and civilian experts from Yugoslavia because they were "surrounded by unfriendliness and treated with hostility."

Tito, who had simply wanted Moscow recognition of his right to independent decision, was stunned by the violence of Stalin's reaction. He wrote Stalin that he was both "surprised and hurt" by the Kremlin directive, and somewhat

plaintively asked "the real reason" for it. A frigid reply came
on March 27, 1948, signed by both Stalin and Molotov and
delivered in person by the sour-faced Soviet Ambassador.

It consisted of eight pages of vitriolic accusation beginning, "We consider your answer untruthful and therefore
wholly unsatisfactory." Tito was shocked. "Scanning the
opening lines," he admitted later, "I felt as if a thunder-
bolt had struck me." After pacing his study and brooding
for hours, he composed an angry reply. From then until
May 22, he and Stalin exchanged a series of biting letters
that steadily widened the rift between them.

Stalin accused him of affronting Red Army commanders;
of tolerating "questionable Marxists" like Djilas and Rankovic in his cabinet; of failing to maintain a revolutionary spirit
in the Yugoslav Communist Party. It was the Red Army, the
Soviet dictator fumed, that had "crushed the German in-
vader, liberated Belgrade, and in this way created the conditions . . . for the YCP to achieve power." So how could
Tito "sink so low" as to fail to show proper gratitude?

Tito refused to admit any heresy. "National and international exigencies," he insisted, "compel us to develop Socialism in our country in a somewhat different form from
that attained in the Soviet Union." He reminded Stalin tartly
that the Partisans had received Soviet help only in the final
weeks of the war; that Stalin had failed to support Yugoslavia's demand for Trieste; that he had tried to sabotage
Tito's industrialization program for Russia's benefit. Was
Stalin so blinded by his own nationalism that he could not
appreciate or respect the nationalism of others?

The master of the Kremlin was dumfounded at Tito's
failure to shrivel under his terrible blasts. It was intolerable
that the Goliath of the Communist world who had purged
every rival, who had triumphed over the mighty Axis powers,
should be defied by a little Balkan David with a slingshot.

Apart from the humiliation, it was a dangerous precedent. If he let Tito get away with it, Moscow would unquestionably face revolts from other little Red leaders with big ideas in East Europe. Tito *must* be crushed!

But how? Stalin gloomily recalled what he had been told about Yugoslav hitchhikers. They would stand right in the middle of traffic with arms outstretched. You either had to pick them up or knock them down; no compromise was possible.

"I will shake my little finger," Stalin growled to Politburo member Nikita Khrushchev, "and there will be no more Tito!" But eight years later Khrushchev was to tell the 20th Communist Party Congress in Moscow ruefully, "We have paid dearly for this shaking of the little finger!"

No Kremlin official at the time dared suggest to Stalin that he was making a terrible blunder, or that there was secret support in the Communist world for Tito's position. Until the war there had been no other Socialist countries with which Stalin had to work out relations; he had no precedent but his own megalomania. He found it impossible to take seriously the challenge of a tiny power like Yugoslavia.

Once Churchill had argued with him about a policy because the Vatican was likely to object. "And how many divisions," Stalin smiled contemptuously, "has the Pope?"

Now he set the wheels in motion for Tito's destruction. Portraits of Tito suddenly disappeared in every country of eastern Europe. Copies of Stalin's letters denouncing him— but not Tito's replies—were sent to all Communist Parties. Every Red capital quickly echoed these attacks.

Tito conferred with Djilas, Kardelj and Rankovic. "If you think I'm an obstacle to good relations with the Soviet Union," he told them soberly, "I'm willing to retire quickly." They rejected his offer indignantly.

Djilas countered, "Old man, if you think it would help if any of *us* resigned, I'm quite ready to do so."

"What the devil should I do if you went?" he growled.

"Stalin has us surrounded nicely," Rankovic sighed.

"Was there ever a time that we were *not* surrounded? We were so before the war, during the war and even now." Tito's chin went up stubbornly. "But we shall break through!"

Stalin was certain, however, that other Yugoslav leaders like Zujovic and Hebrang, loyal to Moscow and chagrined by the danger of losing their ties to the Communist world, would repudiate Tito's heresy. A few worried Politburo members ventured to suggest to Stalin that he might be misreading the temper of most of the men around Tito.

Stalin just smiled sarcastically. "Let him call a full session of the YCP Central Committee. Then we shall see!"

Tito accepted the challenge.

The full Central Committee met in the library of the old palace on April 12, 1948. One after the other, seventeen members rose to support Tito's defiance of Stalin. Then Black Zujovic got up and faced his old war comrade angrily.

"I am against such an attitude," he protested. "How can we convince ourselves and the people that we are on the right path if the Soviet Party and Stalin do not approve?"

Pacing up and down the library, Tito replied, "It hurts to see and hear Zujovic speak as he does, as if to say, 'How dare we pygmies oppose the Soviet Party?' You, Black, have assumed the right to love the Soviet Union more than your country. . . . Comrades, our revolution does not devour its children. The children of *this* revolution are too honest!"

The Committee voted to send Stalin a tactful but firm letter of support for Tito's position. Stalin was outraged. He ordered the Soviet Embassy in Belgrade to consult secretly with Zujovic on anti-Tito moves for the Fifth Yugoslav Party Congress to be held in nine weeks.

Tito learned of the meeting. "Treason!" he muttered.

Zujovic and Hebrang were expelled from the Central Committee and the Party, then arrested and jailed.

Stalin's retaliation was swift and shattering.

The Cominform met in Bucharest on June 28, 1948, a historic date that marked the end of international Communism as a monolithic world power. Yugoslavia was excommunicated from the Communist family of nations, its leaders condemned for "ambition, arrogance and conceit." Specific charges included refusing to obey Cominform edicts; affronting the Soviet Union; not subordinating the peasantry to the proletariat; failing to suppress capitalism; refusing to accept criticism "in a Marxist manner"; adopting "a position of nationalism"; using "terrorism" against Zujovic and Hebrang.

Stalin's blow was no light one. Expulsion from the Cominform meant that Tito no longer had mutual assistance treaties with the other Communist countries of eastern Europe, and could no longer trade with them or Russia. Yugoslavia had depended on this commerce for the oil and cotton imports it needed, and for 50 percent of its exports.

Now Tito stood alone in the world—cast out by the East; without allies in the West. Washington and London, fascinated by this astonishing development, waited to see what would happen next. Would Tito go to the sinners' bench in Moscow to repent and plead for forgiveness? Or would other Red leaders in Yugoslavia now decide to dump him, replacing him with a stooge acceptable to Stalin?

When Tito first read a full account of the Cominform proceedings in a Prague newspaper, he became so angry he went out and shot all the frogs in his pond with a .22

rifle until his fury subsided. Other bad news came quickly. Czechoslovakia began recalling its tourists from Dalmatia, which for generations had been a favorite Czech holiday resort.

But Josip Broz Tito was no man to run from a fight.

Instead of suppressing the Cominform resolution in the Yugoslav press, as Stalin and Red satellite leaders were sure he would, Tito astonished them by ordering it published in full. Along with all the charges made against him, he let the Yugoslav people read his letters to Stalin which the Kremlin boss had suppressed.

"Let them judge for themselves," Tito told Kardelj.

The people did. In a groundswell of Yugoslav indignation against the Soviet Union, the country united behind its leader. "We're a mad bunch, we Yugoslavs," Djilas said to Tito, laughing. "We're only at our best when any big power tries to bully our little country—whether it's Germany invading us, America violating our air space, or the Soviet Union trying to force us to our knees!"

Radio Belgrade announced to the world that Yugoslavia had no intention of knuckling under to the Kremlin. Mosa Pijade sardonically reminded Red leaders who had expelled them from the Cominform that during World War II, while Kremlin bigwigs had remained in Moscow "smoking their pipes and sleeping on mattresses," Tito and his men had fought and bled heroically in battles that had helped save Communism.

Reaction from the Kremlin was violent and swift.

"We possess information," Andrei Zhdanov told the Cominform shrilly, "that Tito is an imperialist spy!"

Inflammatory charges were spread that Tito had had Zujovic murdered in prison. Yugoslav minorities began to be mistreated in Cominform countries and in the Soviet Union. Young Yugoslav officers training in Moscow were urged to mount a coup to overthrow Tito's regime.

With Soviet pressure against him steadily intensifying the West felt sure that Tito's days in power—and on earth —were numbered. Rumors spread that Belgrade was under siege and that he had fled. "Tito got what he deserved," gloated a Mihailovic supporter in London. "We will, if fortune is so kind, never hear from him again!"

There was breathless speculation as the Fifth Party Congress met on July 21, 1948. Would Tito appear? If he did, would the 2,344 delegates from all over Yugoslavia support him or force him out and seek reinstatement in the Cominform, with a lifting of the crippling trade embargo?

When Marshal Josip Broz Tito made his appearance in the congress hall, the delegates gave him a standing ovation. Largely Partisans who had fought through the harsh mountain war with him, they roared their enthusiasm for the leader who had brought them victory, toppled the corrupt monarchy, built a Socialist state in its place, and united them as comrades after centuries of bloody feuding. Should they desert him now just because Stalin condemned his patriotism?

Replying to the vituperation being hurled at him from all the Red capitals of eastern Europe, orchestrated from Moscow, Tito defended himself as a solid Marxist-Leninist.

"We are fully aware of all the things that are spoken and written against us," he declared. "They are painful things, lies, insults, fabrications; but so far from being intimidated by them we have drawn strength from them to hold our ground. . . . We know we are on the right course!"

In a stunning and humiliating setback for Stalin, the Yugoslav Congress voted complete support for Tito, with only a handful of votes against him. The Western world reacted to this dramatic development with intense interest.

Tito's political earthquake had opened a fault in the Balkans. How many other small Red nations would escape through it? Ironically, one independent Communist had done more, singlehandedly, to deal a crushing blow to Stalinism than all the billions of dollars spent by America's Cold War under President Truman. A unique new way to divide world Communism was suddenly suggested to the West— encouraging independence of Moscow by other Communist nations, through a program of Western aid and trade with them.

Vice Premier Wladyslaw Gomulka, head of the Polish Communist Party, was the first to indicate sympathy for Tito's position. At a quick signal from the Kremlin, loyal Stalinists in Poland arrested Gomulka and threw him in jail.

Stalin bitterly upbraided Kremlin officials for not having sent larger Soviet forces into Yugoslavia under Marshal Tolbukhin, and kept them there, no matter how much Tito protested. In all the other countries of eastern Europe, occupation by the Red Army had ensured their subservience to Moscow. Stalin could not invade Yugoslavia now without risking a clash with the United States, which in 1948 was still sole possessor of the atomic bomb.

The loss of Yugoslavia was a severe blow to his military posture, economic plans, prestige and influence. Next to Russia's, Tito's army of thirty divisions was the largest in Europe and the toughest. The only country in Europe that possessed twenty-three out of the twenty-six basic strategic raw materials, Yugoslavia led Europe as a source of lead, bauxite and antimony; was second in producing copper, zinc and mercury.

By emerging as a rival Communist force opposed to Stalinism, Titoism marked the end of an era in which Stalin had been able to use Communism as an extension of Russian imperialism. Tito's rebellion had cracked and seriously weakened Moscow's monopoly of moral authority over Communism, opening the door to a new era of independent Communist movements.

The West was now far safer against any possible attack by a unified world coalition of Communist nations.

The Cominform boycott forced Yugoslavs to tighten their belts. Rationing was introduced. Half-built power plants in construction shut down for lack of Czech machinery. Cherries and plums from Yugoslav orchards that had helped pay for it now withered on the trees for lack of a market.

"I don't know whether we've been politically murdered," Kardelj admitted wryly, "or committed economic suicide!"

"Our ports are still open to western Europe," Tito reminded him hopefully. "There are other countries in the world besides Stalin's satellites!" He was waiting for a reaction to a feeler he had put out to Washington "for re-examination of relations of Eastern-Western trade and commercial relations with the United States."

Tito knew that the only thing that could save them from economic disaster was the decision of the West to come to his rescue. During the war, when Stalin had been deaf to his appeals, the American commander, General Dwight D. Eisenhower, had not. United States supplies had been parachuted to him when he needed them desperately. And after the war UNRRA aid, largely American, had helped feed his starving people.

But the Yugoslavs had been allies then. The Trieste affair, Tito's one-sided elections, the shooting down of United States planes, had since chilled Washington toward Belgrade. The Cold War, furthermore, had made anti-Communism almost a religious crusade in State Department policy.

Tito's plight was not unlike that of Winston Churchill's in "England's finest hour," when the nation stood alone under threat of total destruction by Hitler's Luftwaffe. The United States had come to democratic England's rescue.

Would it do the same to save a Communist Yugoslavia?

"We Are the Equals of the Russians!"

MEANWHILE Tito was being vituperated daily in the Moscow and Red satellite press as a Fascist, murderer, imperialist agent, spy, beast, liar and terrorist. Tito shrewdly avoided making similar personal attacks on Stalin.

"I had to give Stalin time," he explained later, "to behave in such a way that people in Yugoslavia would say 'Down with Stalin' of their own accord, without my having to suggest it to them." By the end of 1948 his restraint had paid off; Stalin's shrill propaganda had backfired badly, uniting all shades of Yugoslav political opinion behind Tito.

The decision to fight Stalin had been one of the most difficult he had ever had to make, but now that he was in the thick of the fight he was glad he had made it. Yugoslav Communists roared with delight when he told them firmly, "In the teachings of Marx, Engels, Lenin and—yes, Stalin himself—we are the equals of the Russians!" He would prove it by building a purely Yugoslav road to Socialism.

"We now know of what our sin consists," he said on December 27, 1948. "It is our desire to build Socialism in a hurry . . . to electrify and industrialize our country, not remain a backward agricultural country that only ships raw materials to other countries in return for manufactures."

Despite his urgent need of United States aid, he was determined not to bend his knee to Washington for it any more than he had to Moscow. American journalist John Gunther put him on the spot by asking whether, if the Cold War came to a hot war, Yugoslavia would fight on the Soviet side.

"Certainly," Tito replied instantly, "because we are *real* Communists." If such a war came, he declared, it would be the Americans who started it and the Russians who won it. Aggressors, like Hitler, usually lost wars. But didn't Tito himself fear an armed attack from Russia? No, he said, "because that would mean the end of Socialism in the world!"

Clearly labeling himself not for sale to any power, East or West, Tito was confident Washington fully appreciated his value to the West as the spoiler of Communist world unity. It was to their advantage to keep Titoism afloat as an example and encouragement to other disaffected Red satellites. United States aid to Tito would show them they didn't have to depend on Moscow to survive as Communist nations. The more Titos, the weaker Soviet control over eastern Europe and Kremlin influence in the world.

On February 18, 1949, he won his gamble. The US National Security Council lifted a secret economic embargo on Yugoslavia and a $20 million loan was authorized. Upset conservatives in Congress were soothed with assurances that in accepting United States aid, Tito would be opening Yugoslavia to Western ideas and influence. Aid to him, meanwhile, was a black eye for the Soviet Union in the Cold War.

The Kremlin immediately accused Tito of "selling out" to capitalism. "If that is what it means to accept United States aid," Tito replied coolly, "then we must ask Comrade Stalin if he sold out to capitalism when he accepted Ameri-

can help to build the Dneprogres Dam." He made it crystal-
clear to Washington that there had to be no political strings
to the aid offered him, or he didn't want it.

"And no conditions of any kind were attached," he acknowledged later to foreign correspondents. "This was a very
good example which has done a great deal for American
policy and prestige. Our people greatly appreciate this gesture. The American government and people will always have
the Yugoslav people on their side in the struggle for peace."

He was especially grateful because a devastating
drought in the summer of 1950 made the loan, plus both
US and UNRRA food shipments, almost a matter of life-
and-death to the Yugoslavs. Tito made certain that when
the United States food was distributed, his people knew the
Americans had sent it.

Warming up to the West, he began to make voluntary
gestures of appreciation. He closed the Yugoslav-Greek
border, an act that had the effect of ending the uprising of
the Greek Communists whose militancy waxed and waned
according to orders from the Kremlin.

Tito knew that Red China deplored the Cominform expulsion of Yugoslavia, and was itself chafing under Stalin's
harsh economic demands. So on October 5, 1949, Tito recognized Mao Tse-tung's regime, hoping that Mao, too, would
decide to break away from Moscow. But the hardening of
United States policy toward Red China kept Mao from making this move.

Stalin's propaganda guns continued to roar out at Tito.
History was freely rewritten with liberal use of Stalin's
favorite phrase, "as is known," which meant, "I don't have
to prove it." A typical blast in the Moscow *Literary Gazette*
of October, 1949, read: "As is known, the coward Tito and
his entourage were spending their time on the island of Vis,
or attending drinking parties with Randolph Churchill . . .
while Marshal Tolbukhin's forces, after annihilating Hitler's

divisions, were occupying Belgrade. . . . The workers have long since discerned the vile and repulsive snout of the Belgrade deserter to the camp of imperialism, the hireling spy and murderer, the bankrupt Fascist traitor to his country and to the cause of Socialism."

Tito read this choice specimen aloud to Mosa Pijade. Then, his blue eyes twinkling, he picked up a 1946 volume of the *Soviet Encyclopedia* and dryly read from it a report of Stalin's award to him of Russia's highest military honor, the Order of Suvorov: " 'Led by Tito, the People's Liberation Army, together with the Red Army, smashed the Germans in 1944. Tito has a brilliant talent for army leadership; he has great personal courage combined with great charm and the talents of an outstanding politician and statesman.' "

He chuckled. "The same man, do you suppose?"

"Please," Pijade muttered, "don't take Stalin so lightly. He doesn't use only verbal bullets."

At Rankovic's insistence, Yugoslav secret police took precautions to protect Tito against the same kind of Cominform assassination that had overtaken Trotsky in Mexico City. Streets where Tito was scheduled to make a public appearance were closed to traffic, and houses along the route searched. His movements were kept secret, his food tasted before he was allowed to eat it. Bodyguards accompanied him everywhere. Foreign correspondents in the cafés of Belgrade and Zagreb were laying odds that Stalin would succeed in having him killed before 1950.

Several unsuccessful attempts on his life apparently were made, but only one was publicly acknowledged. A man named Milosh Brankovic was sentenced to death for plotting to murder Tito and stage a coup d'etat. Twelve Russians in Yugoslavia were also arrested on charges of espionage, tried and convicted. *Time* magazine interviewed Vittorio Vidali, a man identified to them in Trieste as under instructions to assassinate Tito sometime in 1951. "I don't believe in killing opponents of the Soviet Union through my own actions," he denied blandly. "Tito's rotten, reactionary regime will go because the Yugoslav people will demolish it."

What worried Stalin most about Tito at this point was that his example might infect other Red satellite leaders, some of whom he knew yearned to challenge Kremlin authority. Tito had revived the aging Communist monarch's old fears about a Communism which would be anti-Stalin— the dreaded symbol of which had once been Trotskyism. Now Stalin began to purge eastern Europe satraps he suspected of Titoist tendencies.

Among those arrested and executed in the heresy hunt were Party bureaucrat Lazlo Rajak of Hungary, Deputy Prime Minister Traicho Kostov of Bulgaria, and Party Secretary Rudolf Slansky of Czechoslovokia. A fifth of the whole Rumanian Communist Party were expelled, and many executed.

Tito was inclined to believe the rumors that Stalin had been driven over the brink of paranoia. The *Vozhd* had been stunned by disclosures of plotting against him in the Moscow purge trials of the thirties; Tito's defection and defiance had been another severe blow to his sense of security.

Truman's Secretary of State, Dean Acheson, hinted sternly to the Kremlin that if Stalin unleashed any satellite attack on Yugoslavia, the United States would feel compelled to go to Tito's defense, possibly plunging the world into World War III. Britain's Labor Minister, Aneurin Bevan, reinforced that warning: "Any threat to Yugoslavia, who played a heroic part in resistance to Hitler aggression, is naturally of concern to His Majesty's Government." Tito beamed.

Spokesmen for the Cominform protested shrilly, "Tito is mobilizing thousands of men, thus endearing himself to his American masters, who are spreading war hysteria." Tito told United Press correspondents contemptuously, "That is stupid propaganda. Every intelligent man knows that Socialism is not for sale." Failing to crush Tito's revolt, the Cominform lost both its influence and its bite. It met only once after 1949, then disbanded.

The Soviet Union took up the cudgels directly. Marshal Sokolovsky, Soviet Vice Minister of War, vituperated Tito into 1951 as a "trusted slave . . . bloody executioner . . . Judas . . . imperialist agent whose end is near." Tito had had enough.

Denouncing the USSR as imperialistic, undemocratic and bureaucratic, he urged a UN investigation of Stalin's economic warfare against Yugoslavia. He accused Stalin of provoking border attacks by Yugoslavia's satellite neighbors. And he predicted that Red China would follow his example and break with Moscow. Then he really took the gloves off.

On August 16, 1951, Mosa Pijade declared over Radio Belgrade, "In 1936, 1937 and 1938, over three million people were killed in the Soviet Union. They didn't belong to the bourgeoisie. They were Communists. All those who refused to bow their heads to Stalin were murdered under the names of spies, Fascists and Hitlerite agents!"

Tito scored a diplomatic triumph in February, 1953, by persuading Greece and Turkey to join with Yugoslavia in a Balkans mutual defense pact against Russia. One month later his fantastic struggle with Stalin came to a sudden end.

On March 5, 1953, the Goliath in the Kremlin died.

Tito heard the news with mixed feelings—incredulity, awe, some melancholy and nostalgia, then frank relief. The battle, he knew, was over. And he had won.

Stalin's death galvanized the West into diplomatic action in the Balkans. Fearful that Tito might return to the Soviet orbit now that his personal enemy in the Kremlin was gone, London and Washington sought to keep him politically independent by goodwill gestures. British Foreign Secretary Anthony Eden visited him in Belgrade, and invited Tito to London. So he took his first trip to a Western nation since 1944, and was even given a luncheon by the Queen.

"Imagine," Tito told Djilas, laughing, "a Communist who was once a peasant lad in the mountains fighting his brothers for enough bread to stay alive, breaking bread with the Queen of England in Buckingham Palace!"

Tito's new contacts with the West gradually led him to reevaluate his political concepts. He began to feel that neither side of the Cold War possessed any monopoly of wisdom. The West, he felt, was blind to the truths of Socialism. But the East, particularly Russia, was equally blind to the truths of democratic capitalism. Why not, he reflected, combine the best, and reject the worst, of both worlds?

Increasingly, that idea began to inspire his blueprints for the future of Yugoslavia. Belgrade wits called it "capitalism without capitalists." There was general agreement that it was neither Stalinism nor Americanism. Tito also became convinced that, with tolerance, there was no reason why East and West could not live together in peace. American correspondent William L. Ryan asked Mosa Pijade how Tito could claim to be following Lenin, while rejecting Lenin's theory that Communism and capitalism must inevitably clash.

"Things have changed in the three decades since the Bolshevik revolution," Pijade replied. "Nations of the West are moving leftward, too. There is a possibility that instead of clashing, they will one day come together in common agreement." World peace, not world class struggle, became a cornerstone of the Titoists' foreign policy.

Now that Stalin was dead, Tito held out an olive branch to the Russians—but on his own stiff terms. "We in Yugoslavia would be happy," he declared, "if they openly admitted their mistake toward this country. . . . We are passionately waiting for that!" It was as though Martin

Luther had offered to reconcile with the Vatican if the Pope admitted his guilt in casting Luther out of the Church. But Tito had reason to feel cocky. Stalin's successors were already beginning to talk about "Comrade" Tito in the Soviet press.

American liberals, too, were becoming greatly impressed with Tito's original brand of Communism. On May 13, 1953, former US Ambassador to India Chester Bowles expressed the prophetic hope that Red China, like Yugoslavia, would one day "drift away from Moscow to a more independent position." Eleanor Roosevelt, visiting Belgrade that April, was deeply impressed by a long talk she had with Tito.

"The experiment in Yugoslavia is not Communism," she reported, "and has nothing to do with what Tito calls Soviet imperialism." She felt that, unlike Stalin, Tito had a more modest view of his own role on the world stage. "An intelligent man cannot accept the theory that personalities create history," he told her. "In my opinion, men make history and play a considerable part in it only if they understand the people's needs and wishes, and insofar as they become part of the people themselves."

The violent diatribes against Tito from Moscow and Red satellite capitals suddenly ceased, like water shut off from a tap. Moscow and Belgrade exchanged ambassadors. The newly emerging strong man of the USSR, ebullient Nikita Khrushchev, welcomed the new Yugoslav Ambassador to Moscow with an enthusiastic toast to "Comrade Tito." But the Belgrade diplomat made it carefully plain that Comrade Tito intended to preserve Yugoslavia's independence and neutrality.

"Whatever changes the Soviet Union may make in its foreign policy," Tito firmly assured Associated Press correspondents in Belgrade in August, 1953, "Yugoslavia can never return to her former attitude of cooperation with the

Soviet Union, regardless of whether they are in the interests of our country."

He shrewdly realized that he was now in a uniquely powerful position, eagerly courted by both East and West. But he would lose that power if he cast his lot with one side or the other. On the other hand, tiny Yugoslavia would be in danger of being crushed between the two hostile giants if, singlehanded, it sought to keep them apart.

A new plan occurred to him. Why not keep both forces waiting hopefully in his anteroom while he organized and led a new *third* world force—neutrals who would keep world peace by standing with him between the two great powers?

Excited by the idea, Tito set out on a trip through Asia to line up charter members. In India, after enjoying the thrills of a tiger hunt, he and Prime Minister Nehru issued a joint statement on December 23, 1953, denouncing the policy of power blocs, and calling for "nonalignment" of all uncommitted nations to compel peaceful coexistence between the US and the USSR. "This would not be a third bloc," Tito denied to the editor of the *Hindustani Standard*, "but an expression of world democratic opinion."

Chou En-Lai, Red China's Foreign Minister, also agreed to support Tito's new third force policy. Tito urged the West to recognize Red China "if for no other reason than to give it a chance to demonstrate if it could operate free of Moscow's control." The globe-trotting Marshal crowned his successes by a friendship pact with Afghanistan, then worked out a new trade agreement with the Soviet Union that ended his economic dependence upon the West.

Returning home, he made it clear, however, that he would not join any Red move against the United States. "The Western powers," he declared, "proved in most difficult times to be not our enemies but our friends. . . . We cannot allow the good relations which we have built up with them to deteriorate, simply in order to improve our relations with the countries of the Eastern bloc." Washington was less pleased, however, when he proved his neutrality by also criticizing NATO.

He called the Atlantic Alliance "an American system" of militarism in Europe that might have been justified against Stalin, but not against the new Soviet regime which, Tito believed, was sincerely interested in coexistence. Tito also criticized the United States for aggressive moves to support Chiang Kai-shek on Formosa against Red China. "The people of Asian countries recognize that United States aggression on China's territory of Taiwan," he warned, "endangers peace in Asia and the whole world."

Such criticism was highly displeasing to Americans who felt, like the new Secretary of State, John Foster Dulles, that any world leader who wasn't pro-American, or who was neutral, must be pro-Soviet. George Meany, head of the AFL-CIO, denounced business leaders who sought increased trade with Tito, calling Nehru and Tito "aides and allies" of Communism. Mrs. Roosevelt challenged this view, reminding Meany that "there are areas of the world where Communism means something different from what it does here."

She urged patience, understanding and efforts to bring greater freedom and improvements to any Communist nation open to change like Yugoslavia. President Eisenhower agreed. His requests for foreign aid budgets, however, were cut sharply by Senator William Knowland who, like Dulles, fiercely opposed aid to all nations neutral in the Cold War.

On May 26, 1955, a glorious day for Josip Broz Tito, a Moscow airliner touched down at Belgrade Airport bringing the new Kremlin boss, Nikita Khrushchev, accompanied by Premier Nikolai Bulganin, trade chief Anastas Mikoyan and Foreign Minister Andrei Gromyko, on what could only be described as a penitent mission of apology.

Khrushchev, soon to denounce Stalin himself in far more

violent terms than Tito had, hinted that he himself was a "Titoist" who had never dared reveal his true sentiments while Stalin lived. He expressed sincere regret for the "charges and insults directed against the leaders of Yugoslavia."

Assuring Tito that this unhappy period had now been buried with Stalin, he described the new Soviet regime as ready to "eliminate all obstacles standing in the way of complete normalization" of Yugoslav-Soviet relations. He even told the jubilant Marshal, "The desire of Yugoslavia to maintain relations with all states both in the West and in the East has met with complete understanding on our part."

And he went on to admit that every nation had the right to choose its own road to Socialism, as Tito insisted.

Tito could scarcely believe his ears. The mighty Soviet Union saying it had been wrong, eating humble pie in public, acknowledging his right to Communist independence!

Red satellite leaders in eastern Europe were equally astonished, and began reassessing their own need to genuflect to Moscow. Open revolt simmered in February, 1956, when Khrushchev publicly assailed the crimes of Stalin in a sensational three-hour speech to the 20th Party Congress in Moscow. He blistered Stalin's treatment of Tito as "shameful."

But if Tito had been right, after all, in his successful fight against Soviet domination, then why shouldn't *any* Red leader of eastern Europe follow his example?

14

Titoism
Blows the Lid Off

RETURNING Khrushchev's visit, Tito was greeted in Moscow by huge crowds roaring their delight with the plucky little Balkan rebel who had defied Stalin and gotten away with it, and whose battle for independence seemed to have inspired a new spirit of freedom in the Communist world. In Stalingrad a quarter of a million people broke through police lines to acclaim him. Tito was overwhelmed with emotion.

It seemed only yesterday that he had been an obscure prisoner-of-war on a railway gang in the Urals, where three Cossacks had given him thirty lashes with their knouts. "What amazing changes of fortune time brings!" he marveled to Kardelj.

He returned to Belgrade triumphantly with Khrushchev's eager offer to cancel Yugoslavia's $90 million trade debt to the USSR. Dulles promptly flew to Yugoslavia to offer Tito cancellation of a $100 million United States debt, plus $40 million in new economic aid, provided Tito would join him in calling for freedom for Russia's satellites in eastern Europe.

The Balkan leader agreed, but only to a carefully worded statement that "the east European states should suffer no interference in their internal affairs." In Dulles' eyes that meant interference by Russia. In Tito's view it meant interference by Russia *and* the United States. To make certain that both Dulles and Khrushchev understood his neutrality, he declared, "I am convinced that the Soviets wish peace—just like the Americans do." And he emphasized, "We take from both East and West the things that are positive—and we shall continue to do so. . . . Yugoslavia constitutes, in a certain sense, a bridge between East and West, and I think it is much better to be a bridge than a chasm!"

He made it clear that he did not subscribe to Karl Marx's predictions of doom for capitalism. "Marx could not anticipate the level of development that has been reached in America," he declared in July, 1955. He also felt that stiff income taxes on the American rich, as well as Socialist policies in Britain, showed the flexibility of modern capitalism in moving toward social justice in Western societies.

But how flexible was Tito's Communism in allowing some Western-style personal freedom in his own society? "You have only to go into the countryside or elsewhere to hear people criticizing freely," he assured foreign journalists. "We are not afraid of criticism and we don't stifle it. And we openly admit it when we have made a mistake."

Christian Science Monitor correspondent Eric Bourne found this to be largely true, with Yugoslavs feeling free to crack jokes at Tito's expense. But *New York Times* reporter Jack Raymond found cases of some who had gone to jail for complaints against the government or criticism of its leaders.

He agreed, however, that Tito did not run a police state. "A better idea of what freedom is like in Yugoslavia can be had," he reported, "if one recalls one-party, machine-ridden towns and cities in America." He also found no interest by

Yugoslavs in world revolution, but only in making their own Communist society work well.

Speculating about the world significance of Titoism, Supreme Court Justice William O. Douglas wrote, "Russia of the next generation may, indeed, have the mellowness of present-day Communist Yugoslavia. If Asia industrializes and produces a Genghis Khan with the hydrogen bomb, Russia and America might become indispensable to each other if either is to survive." The date of that remarkable prophecy: 1955.

Khrushchev dissolved the Cominform in April, 1956, and joined Tito in a joint declaration that it was, indeed, possible for different Communist countries to pursue "different roads to Socialism." Tito would have been less than human if he had not thoroughly enjoyed this double vindication. Red leaders from all over Europe, who had ostracized him on Stalin's orders, now hurried to Belgrade to make amends.

Titoism began to blow the lid off eastern Europe in June. A Polish workers' demonstration in Poznan for independence turned into a bloody two-day clash with police and troops, who killed 50 people and wounded 300. An alarmed Khrushchev ringed Warsaw with Soviet tanks to prevent a full-scale uprising. Then he hastily ordered the release from jail of former Red leader Wladyslaw Gomulka, still in jail for "Titoism." Gomulka agreed to head a new Communist regime to restore order if Khrushchev acknowledged his right to pursue "a Polish way" toward Socialism. He won his demand.

On October 23, 1956, two days after Gomulka took power in Poland, Hungary blew up. "Freedom fighters," organized like Tito's Partisans of old, stormed through Budapest toppling Stalin's huge statue, pulling down the red star on top of Parliament, seizing a government radio station. Soviet tanks smashed into the city to crush the rebellion.

"When it comes to fighting imperialists," Khrushchev roared angrily, "we are *all* Stalinists!" Appealing to the West against the Soviet invasion, Premier Imre Nagy took refuge in the Yugoslav Embassy. He was given safe conduct to Belgrade, but was seized en route by Russian secret police who kidnapped him and took him to Rumania. The uprising collapsed.

Tito knew that Khrushchev was now furious with him, blaming him as the cause of all the unrest in eastern Europe. He persisted, nevertheless, in using a balancing pole to walk the tightrope over the chasm between East and West.

"We are against the intervention and use of foreign military power," he declared flatly in November, 1956. But then he argued ingeniously that the swift Soviet suppression of the Hungarian rebellion had been a "lesser evil" than the Third World War that might have resulted if the chaos in Hungary had led to a direct clash between East and West. "Intervention was a mistake; but war would be a catastrophe!"

Khrushchev angrily cut off credits to Yugoslavia, and Moscow–Belgrade relations chilled once more. Tito refused to attend the 40th Anniversary celebration of the Bolshevik Revolution in Moscow. In 1958 he resumed his trips overseas to strengthen ties with uncommitted leaders of his third force—Nasser of Egypt, Nehru of India, Sukarno of Indonesia, U Nu of Burma, Abdullah Khalil of the Sudan.

In Washington, still convinced that neutrality was "immoral," Dulles was grimly disapproving. But President Eisenhower took a different view. "Tito is in a far different position with respect to the free world than are Communist countries that are directly controlled by Communism," he declared. "It is international Communism that spells the greatest danger. . . . Independent Communism is something else."

Tito remained just as critical of United States foreign policy as he was of the Kremlin's. In the October, 1957, issue of the American periodical *Foreign Affairs,* he pointed out that if Stalin had been chiefly responsible for the Cold War up to his death, it was Washington that had intensified it since.

"Establishing military bases in Europe, the Middle East and Asia involves a constant danger to peace," he warned, adding, "The Soviet leaders look upon this, rightly in my opinion, as a policy of encirclement, a threat of war and an aggressive attempt to isolate the Soviet Union."

A few years later he also took the United States to task for interfering in the internal affairs of Cuba, Venezuela and the Dominican Republic on behalf of the wealthy classes.

He vigorously championed the Soviet's proposal for total world disarmament. Discounting its rejection by the United States on grounds of Soviet refusal to inspections, Tito felt that the real reason was an American dread that drastic disarmament would provoke a severe business depression and unemployment.

"What strange logic!" he declared in a speech in April, 1960. "Would an economic crisis be provoked by using $120 billion for productive purposes, for employing millions of workers in production, for peaceful purposes, for assistance to underdeveloped countries?" A year later he pleaded again that delay in nuclear disarmament, particularly, was unforgivable. "Do we not run the risk," he warned, "that an irresponsible lunatic might endanger all of mankind?"

Now in his late sixties, Tito remained an astonishing picture of health—muscular, clear-sighted, hair full, teeth sparkling white, mentally and physically vigorous. He took obvious pleasure in eating well, dressing with flair and enjoying every luxury at a castle in Slovenia and villa on Brioni, where he rode, hunted and swam. He married again in 1952.

His third wife, Jovanka Budisavjelic, was a dark, attractive Serbian woman who had also fought as a Partisan.

He never made the mistake of isolating himself from his people, frequently traveling through the country to talk directly to peasants and workers and listen to their complaints and wishes. "Those talks teach me," he told his friend Vladimir Dedijer, "what needs to be done. I also learn a great deal from people who visit me from all over the world."

Visitors now found him as tough and shrewd as ever, but mellowed somewhat with the years, his outlook broader, far more concerned with human values than with Communist theory, and always ready to laugh. President Eisenhower met him for the first time at the UN in September, 1960.

"He was shorter than I expected, and reserved," Eisenhower recalled. "In contrast to Khrushchev, he was a good listener. I felt he could have profited much from a trip around our country. . . . He seemed anxious to convince me that Yugoslavia was not on the best terms with all members of the Communist bloc. . . . [He] made quite a point of the affection that the Yugoslavs feels for the United States because of our help to them during World War II."

Tito had even more reason to feel appreciative; by this time he had received over a billion dollars in United States economic aid, more than Washington had given to all of Latin America. Eisenhower was understandably irked when Tito once more proved his independence by accepting new friendly overtures from Khrushchev at the UN when they met there, and supporting many Soviet positions. "Yugoslavia is neutral," Khrushchev crowed, "but I believe it would fight on the Soviet side if the USSR were attacked." Tito received no invitation to visit Washington during his stay on American soil, a direct snub.

He shrugged. No bribes or pressure or cajolery or threats or snubs, from Moscow or Washington, would ever pry him loose from his own stubborn brand of Communist neutrality. Tito now had only two criteria for judging an issue. Which side did he honestly believe was right? Which side was more likely to keep the world at peace? In September, 1961, he played host in Belgrade to a conference of neutral nations attended by India, Burma, Indonesia, Egypt, Cuba and others.

A new American President, John F. Kennedy, wanted to send them a message of good wishes, to show the world's nonaligned nations that the old Dulles policy of intolerance for neutrality was dead; that the "New Frontier" respected any nation's right not to take sides in the Cold War.

Outraged State Department bureaucrats tried to stop the President's message, but he sent it anyway. Hamilton Fish Armstrong, editor of *Foreign Affairs*, reported that it had greatly impressed and favorably influenced the Belgrade Conference, and that the President had been right. Failure to send it would have been a major diplomatic blunder.

Visiting Tito after the Belgrade Conference, Supreme Court Justice Douglas probed his sincerity as a neutral once more by asking him—for publication—a key question: "If Russian armies were withdrawn from the eastern European nations, would you expect changes in five or ten years?" No secret Soviet sympathizer could go on record as admitting that the Red Army was enforcing Communism on eastern Europe.

"In five or ten years?" Tito replied without hesitation. "Why, there would be changes *at once!*"

During the Cuban crisis early in 1963, some American papers headlined a rumor that American planes sold to Yugoslavia were being used in Cuba. The truth was that Castro had asked Tito for planes but had been turned down. "No aid I get from America has been or will be used against America," Tito declared firmly. "Yes, we recognize Cuba and have an ambassador there, just as we have in almost all nations of the world. But Cuba looks with the same distrust upon 'Tito the revisionist' as Khrushchev does!"

"One of these days," an American columnist observed ironically, "Washington is going to wake up to the fact that Tito the Communist is not in the Kremlin's pocket. And Moscow is going to realize that Tito the rebel is no American stooge. Then both will understand what he has been trying to tell them for almost a quarter of a century. *Tito the Yugoslav is for Yugoslavia!*"

Just being for Yugoslavia was complicated enough.

The Yugoslav Communist Party was splintered into two groups. One wanted the Central Committee to retain an iron grip on the government: the classic dictatorship of the proletariat. The other insisted that the Party "wither away," as Lenin had predicted, turning more and more functions over to the people themselves and their local committees.

Tito listened to both sides thoughtfully. The question was one of timing. *When,* actually, was it time for dictatorship to mellow and phase out for direct popular control?

He moved cautiously to avoid precipitating a Party split that might flare into civil war, exacerbated by old nationalist rivalries. His thorniest problem was his old friend and comrade Milovan Djilas, who espoused the wing of the YCP devoted to free speech and democracy. In 1951 Djilas had declared enthusiastically, "From now on the Party line is that there is *no* Party line!" He was wholeheartedly behind Tito's liberal reforms a year earlier that turned over factories and mines to workers to manage through their own committees. But Tito worried about too much democracy too soon.

Tito felt compelled to act when two thousand peasant families, hearing that it was possible to emigrate, swamped

the American Embassy in Belgrade with requests for visas
in 1951 to escape age-old poverty aggravated by war and
droughts. Djilas was outraged when some applicants were
jailed on trumped-up charges, to discourage large-scale emi-
gration. Tito admitted on June 26 that he was compelled to
be repressive "because of our poverty," but insisted the situation was only temporary. To pacify the peasants, he ordered
an immediate stop to all efforts to force them to join collec-
tives.

He had to admit that the collective program had been a
dismal failure. When the government had imported 3,500
pedigreed English pigs to improve the breed, Serbian collec-
tives had been given 3,000, Croatian peasants 500. In six
months there were no English pigs left in Serbia. But in
Croatia, where peasants had taken the pigs into their own
cottages and treated them like "family," the original 500
had multiplied dramatically, with their pedigrees kept pure.
Serbs were forced to buy English pedigreed pigs on the
Croatian market, at five times the price of ordinary porkers.

Djilas also grew gradually disillusioned by what he considered sabotage of Tito's industrial reforms. In 1953 he
lashed out at Party bureaucrats for compelling regional trade
unions to take their orders from Belgrade, despite the fact
that they were supposed to control their own local factories.
"If the revolution is to survive," Djilas warned, "it must
transform itself into democracy and Socialism!"

The outraged Central Committee bureaucracy accused
Djilas of having sold out to Western capitalism, and ordered
him to stop his attack on them. He refused. The Committee
unanimously demanded his arrest and trial. To prevent a
dangerous split with his followers, Tito reluctantly agreed.

On January 16, 1954, Djilas was tried openly in a Belgrade District Court with the foreign press present and the
proceedings broadcast to the country. He was permitted to

answer his accusers and make an opening and closing statement. Found guilty, he was stripped of all his Party and
government titles and functions, and retired to his home as
a private citizen. He lived freely in Belgrade, receiving all
foreign and local visitors who called on him.

But it was as impossible to silence the impetuous, uncompromising Djilas as Stalin had found it to subdue Tito.

Interviewed in November by an Austrian correspondent,
he blasted the YCP as having become "reactionary," and
charged, "Stalinism of a domestic type has taken over in
Yugoslavia!" Infuriated, Marko Rankovic demanded that
Djilas be put in jail. Tito refused. Djilas continued his attacks.

The Yugoslav people, Djilas insisted, were ready to
support the regime under more democratic conditions if they
were just trusted and given a chance. They would certainly
vote for Tito, if not for the Party bureaucrats—especially
police boss Rankovic. Djilas also blamed Party sloth for the
fact that 1956 per capita income was only $110 annually,
with three out of four Yugoslavs still chained to farms
despite Tito's avowed goal of all-out industrialization.

He took a swing at Tito, too, for not having flatly condemned Khrushchev's armed intervention in Hungary.
Rankovic warned grimly that "Djilasism" had brought the
YCP and the country to the boiling point. Tito reluctantly
let Djilas be jailed on a charge of slandering Yugoslavia in his
writings which were "intended to . . . undermine the effect
of Yugoslav foreign policies." But even prison couldn't silence
Tito's fiery ex-Vice President and onetime heir apparent.

Far from showing repentance, Djilas wrote a book about
his disillusionment with Yugoslav Communism, *The New
Class*, and smuggled it out of jail for American publication.
In it he revealed that he had hoped in vain that Tito's revolution would bring about a true Socialist democracy, because

he distrusted Communist power. "I was never really comfortable with it," he confessed, "and I don't think I ever could be!"

Meanwhile, prodded by Djilas' charges, Tito began to investigate blunders of the Party bureaucracy. He was shocked to discover that families were being thrown into the street for moving into apartments or building their own houses without permits. "No upholding of legality," he blistered officials responsible, "can justify the expulsion into the snow and cold of families with small children!"

He found bureaucratic blunders in his experiments at blending Socialism and private enterprise. Prospering "little capitalists"—barbers, blacksmiths, bakers, shoemakers, tailors —had had their taxes raised by 700 percent. When 10,000 shops were driven out of business, Yugoslavs found it impossible to get plumbers, electricians, or their shoes repaired in less than a month.

Tito introduced economic reforms that produced a steady improvement in living conditions. Clothes became cheaper, with more and better food available at lower prices. When a rash of strikes broke out in April, 1964, he ordered wages raised and workers' grievances satisfied. In full sympathy with the peasant's love of his own land, Tito stopped the Central Committee's attempt to speed up collectivization, which still provided only 20 percent of Yugoslavia's food.

He was helped to sustain private enterprise on the farms by a United States–Yugoslav "Food for Peace" program, which sold him American agricultural products on generous credit terms. President Kennedy, who had invited Tito to the White House in October, 1963, had assured him of this aid and of the new Administration's firm respect for his right to be neutral. He was greatly impressed with the President as an intelligent young leader seeking original answers to old problems.

News of Kennedy's assassination saddened him. After a moving tribute to the late President over Radio Belgrade, Tito went to the American Embassy in person to pay his respects. Then he ordered all Yugoslav flags flown at half-mast, and instructed the nation's schoolteachers to devote an hour in class to discussing Kennedy's achievements.

It was a remarkable salute from a tough old Communist.

"Very Clever, the Old Man Is!"

STALIN's death brought a second important defection from the Kremlin camp—Red China. At first Tito was delighted to see another Communist country assert its independence. But he was soon shocked at Mao Tse-tung's apparent readiness to risk a thermonuclear war with the capitalist world, a policy Tito considered "insane, utterly inhumane and anti-Socialist." In 1964 he aligned himself with both the United States and the USSR against Red China's aggressive policies.

World peace and Socialism, Tito insisted, were inseparable. He urged Mao to join the third force in the UN for peaceful coexistence, "since there is no other way, unless all of us are to perish completely." He privately felt that the Chinese were overestimating their role in world affairs.

His own prestige and influence soared steadily. The Rumanian government, encouraged by Tito, began to follow in his footsteps, pursuing a course increasingly independent of Moscow. By 1967 the Rumanians had achieved so much self-determination that even the United States agreed to support its Communist delegate to the UN as the new Secretary-General. The Czechs, too, followed Tito's lead in Socialist reform, to such an extent that by 1968 they had almost transformed their country back into the democracy it once had been.

But Tito's unique brand of Socialism began to run into serious trouble at home in 1965, when 230 strikes crippled the economy. Wages were raised, but inflation set in, with the cost of living soaring 13 percent in a single year. A 7 percent unemployment rate also sent 80,000 Yugoslavs to West Germany in search of jobs. Factory workers complained that salesmen earned eight times as much as they were paid.

Each section of the country began demanding that costly industrial plants be built in its own province, exactly as American states seek government projects for their own regions. Tito gave the highest priority to the development of the three poorest republics—Bosnia-Herzegovina, Macedonia and Montenegro. The wealthier republics grumbled at being taxed for this purpose, but Tito was determined to develop the country with economic equality for all Yugoslavs.

Like Djilas, who had been sacrificed to appease the bureaucrats on the Central Committee, Tito, too, wanted to liberalize Yugoslav Communism. But all through 1965 he found his economic reforms persistently opposed and sabotaged by Marko Rankovic, who had been made Vice President in place of Djilas. A Kremlin favorite, Rankovic was known as "little Tito," and was considered the Party official most likely to succeed Tito. Still holding on to his police powers, he began purging liberal Party officials who opposed him.

The pattern was painfully familiar to Tito; he wanted no Joseph Stalins in the country he loved. He threw a bombshell into Party ranks by suddenly stripping Rankovic of his government and Party posts. "I am really sorry that it came to this," he told the Central Committee. "Marko spent a lot of time with me. He grew up under my wing, so to speak.

But when it comes down to it, the Party, the people and the country, are more important than one individual!"

He charged Rankovic with having made the state security service into "a system which has put our entire society under oppression." UDBA police had arrested people without stating charges, and held them incommunicado for months. Rankovic had admitted himself that 47 percent of UDBA arrests in 1949 had been illegal, 23 percent involving only minor offenses. Tito had curbed their power with a revised Criminal Code in 1951, but Rankovic had refused to abide by it.

It was whispered in Belgrade that Tito had finally cracked down after discovering that Rankovic had dared to plant a secret wire-tap in the Presidential residence. But Tito's chief reason for not having taken action sooner was his worry that a purge of the largely Serbian secret service might touch off the ancient feud between Serbs and Croats.

Leadership positions in the Party and government were topheavy with Serbs, who made up two fifths of the population, compared to the better-educated, more highly skilled Croats, who constituted a fourth, and the 9 percent of Slovenes. The other 26 percent of the Yugoslav melting pot consisted of Macedonians, Montenegrins, Albanians, Bulgarians, Greeks, Hungarians and Turks—all united under Tito largely by the force of his magnetic personality.

He was ruefully aware that the ranks of the old war comrades around him had thinned steadily until now only Edvard Kardelj was left. Mosa Pijade was dead; the others were either banished from power or in jail. Tito was unhappiest about the imprisonment of Milovan Djilas. He had repeatedly urged Djilas to recant his attacks on the regime, so that Tito could free him, but Djilas wouldn't. In 1961 Tito had paroled him anyway, whereupon Djilas promptly published another book in America, *Conversations with Stalin*.

Opening old Soviet-Yugoslav wounds, it brought a roar

of outraged protests from Moscow. Back to jail went Djilas, his parole revoked for "disclosing official secrets." But in 1966 Tito's conscience compelled him to free the stubborn Montenegrin once more. Belgrade wits laughed, "Stalin had his Tito; now Tito has his Djilas!"

Sensitive to rising discontent with the rigid bureaucracy of the Central Committee, Tito tried to work out an adroit compromise. Power was divided between an old guard Senate of thirty-five "leading personalities," with himself as President, and a streamlined Party Executive Committee dominated by young liberals. The Senate would lay down broad government objectives; but the Executive Committee would decide how, when and where to implement them. The result was a sharp upswing in the degree of self-government in Yugoslavia.

Tenant Councils began to run their own apartment houses; Worker Councils their own plants. Industries had to justify their management by showing a profit. More planning and taxing was done at the local level, with the man in the street given a greater voice in his own affairs.

As the Yugoslav economy began to boom, Tito told US Supreme Court Justice Douglas, "We want no gifts, no charity. We want to pay for all we get." He was particularly eager for greater technical assistance. "It gives us a chance to train our engineers and technicians in America. We need that help badly." Most unemployed in Yugoslavia were unskilled workers living in undeveloped areas.

Justice Douglas, returning after a ten-year absence, found that Tito's crash program of industrialization had changed his 75 percent peasant nation to one with a balanced economy, in which 50 percent of the people worked in factories.

Per capita income had jumped from $110 to $400, plus about $100 in social security benefits providing accident, health, unemployment and burial insurance. There were also

rent subsidies, child allowances for each child under fourteen, free schooling up to and including the university and
retirement pensions starting at age fifty.

The average worker or farmer of Yugoslavia has a long
way to go before he is as well off as his counterpart in the
United States. But compared to the life his father led under
the old monarchy, he is living in paradise.

Still remarkably fit and vigorous in 1968, the seventy-six-
year-old Yugoslav leader impresses visitors as a tough, hearty,
charming man with an engaging sense of humor. He betrays
his age only by taking hourly recesses during his three-hour
speeches. Living in splendid semiretirement, he shuttles between his various palaces in Belgrade, the island of Brioni
and the Julian Alps. An early riser—5:30 A.M. in summer,
7:00 A.M. in winter—he does Swedish exercises for half an
hour, shaves, goes for a brisk walk regardless of the weather.
After a light breakfast at eight, he feeds his canaries
and goes to his office. He scans the morning papers, especially letters to the editor, and reviews verified letters of
complaint from citizens against bureaucrats. Nine times out
of ten he orders corrective action. He studies news bulletins
and pending legislation, though he prefers leaving domestic
policy to his newly rejuvenated government. Concentrating
on diplomacy, he examines the foreign press for clues to im-
pending world developments.

Receiving Yugoslav officials and delegates and overseas
visitors, he is also never too busy for an old school chum,
villager or revolutionary who "knew him when."

Still an ardent book-lover, he likes to relax with Balzac,
Stendhal, Goethe, Dreiser, Jack London, Upton Sinclair or
Sinclair Lewis. If his mood is for music, he prefers Strauss,
Beethoven and Tchaikovsky, or he may play the accordion
himself. He delights in a good chess game, and enjoys putter-
ing in his workshop at metalwork, the craft at which he once

earned a living while plotting revolution. At times he will
ride through the forest on a favorite horse, dreaming of the
brave old days of Partisan derring-do.

At last reports, five of his brothers and sisters were still
alive. One brother was a retired railway worker; one a peasant; one a janitor. One sister was the wife of a peasant, one of
a shoemaker. Some thought the Broz family's famous brother
heartless because he never used his power to advance their
stations in life. But Tito, opposed to nepotism, refused to feed
relatives at the public trough.

Tito's third wife, Jovanko, looks after him as if he were
a national treasure, seeing to it that he has every indulgence
his luxury-loving heart desires. Most Yugoslavs agree that he
is a national treasure, deserving of any reward he craves. "A
great many Yugoslavs continue to think of Tito as an authen-
tic national hero," observed journalist John Gunther. Even a
correspondent for the anti-Communist magazine *East Europe*
admitted, "There can be little doubt that Tito enjoys great
popularity among the masses. . . . 'He is very clever, the old
man is,' was a comment I heard frequently when discussion
turned on the aging Marshal."

One American reporter was told proudly by a Belgrade
machinist, "This Tito of ours is a *real* Yugoslav—he shows
how superior we are to Bulgars, Hungarians and Albanians!"

Tito's detractors accuse him of having, like his old enemy Stalin, artificially cultivated his popularity through a
"cult of personality." Journalist Leigh White pointed out
that his picture hung with Lenin's in all classrooms, and that
schoolchildren were compelled to recite this catechism:

> You ask, who is Tito? . . .
> He was born of an angry father and the people. . . .
> You ask, who is Tito?
> Write, my darling machine-gun, write "Tito"!
> Tito is the army, the earth and the river!

No less than any other system, Tito's Communism has had its share of failures. There are still poverty, drabness, long queues for consumer goods, inflated prices, a shortage of vacant apartments. Unemployment and black markets exist. But Tito has never tried to throw up a smoke screen around these embarrassments. He lets foreigners in to see for themselves, and does not attempt to deny what they see.

Unlike most Communist dictators, Tito also allows Yugoslav citizens to travel abroad freely, not at all fearful they might be "contaminated" or seduced by Western life. They are also exposed to contact with millions of tourists who flock to Yugoslavia's beautiful beaches every summer.

Some 300,000 Yugoslavs are at present traveling or working in West Germany, France and other Western nations. Yugoslav artists and writers are free to fraternize with, and be influenced by, artists and writers of the West. The Yugoslav public is free to enjoy Donald Duck, Tarzan, Hemingway, Françoise Sagan and popular Western idols. Remarkably well informed, Yugoslavs are able to discuss international problems, paintings, cars and football matches. They are also exposed to Western-style soap and soft drink ads.

Western visitors are often surprised at the extent to which Yugoslavs speak their minds freely, criticizing aspects that annoy them. "Yugoslavs laugh not only at others but at themselves," Justice Douglas has observed. "In this respect also, they are like Americans. And the Yugoslavs—unlike any Communist group in the world—also laugh at times at Communism."

Tito sees his principal role today as that of peacemaker. When the Arab-Israel conflict broke out in the spring of 1967, he followed the Soviet lead in blaming Israel for taking the offensive; but also flew to Cairo to pressure Nasser into agreeing to negotiate with Israel for a peace settlement.

The two Americans Tito most admires are Justice

Douglas and Ambassador-at-Large Averell Harriman. Douglas encouraged Americans to think of Communism as being as differentiated as democratic capitalism—as different, for example, as a business-oriented America, a Socialist-minded Britain, a nationalist-minded France. And as capable of change. "The shades of gray multiply as Russia moves to the right of China," he explained, "and as Yugoslavia continues to move to the right of Russia."

Foreign diplomats and correspondents acknowledge that Tito could easily win any free election today. Why, then, doesn't he try? First of all, he doesn't have to. Secondly, free elections would require permission for opposition political parties to operate; and Tito does not believe in "fractional strife"—i.e., he wants no challenge to Communist power or planning. Thirdly, it is probably true that without his strong hand at the helm, Yugoslavia might not have survived as a nation. A bitter struggle for power among the six rival nationalities might well have pulled the country apart, as France was fractured before DeGaulle took power.

Finally, Tito takes a cynical Communist view of American-style elections, which he considers a fraudulent choice between two major parties controlled by a bourgeois class and press, neither reflecting the real interests of the great mass of workers and small farmers. In Tito's honest opinion, the YCP speaks for *all* the people . . . but paradoxically, he can't prove this conviction until he consents to free elections. He has, however, sharply increased democracy within Party ranks, to make the popular voice louder. It will never be loud enough for the West until Yugoslavs have the opportunity to vote for a complete change of government if they want it.

If it is a mistake to write Tito off as "just another Red dictator," it is equally a mistake to glorify him as a golden boy of the Balkans. He has made his full share of blunders. He has been inconsistent; he has backed and filled between

East and West in his effort to be "balanced"; he has permitted blunders in economic policy at home.

But overall he has been a remarkably successful Communist leader, moving deliberately in a liberal direction,
steadily improving the lives of his people. He has been
flexible enough to bow to the passionate Yugoslav love of
independence and proud regionalism. His reforms have de-
centralized the country's economy and political structure,
giving every citizen a share in controlling his own fate
through workers' and tenants' councils. Tito laughed uproari-
ously when he heard a Yugoslav journalist moan in despair,
"Reforms, reforms, reforms! How long can it go on?" As long
as Tito is alive, they will never stop. *Newsweek*'s Belgrade
correspondent noted, "The most daring reforms of all are
still ahead."

If Tito's persistent reforms continue until his death, and
are carried forward by his successors, the YCP will probably
be the first Communist Party in the world to fulfill Marx's
prophecy of withering away to let the people rule themselves
in a "true" Communism. Irrepressibly optimistic, Tito persists
in "dreaming the impossible dream."

"The Communist Party cannot continue to function in
the same way if at the same time the state is withering away,"
he insists. "Many of our people do not realize this fact yet.
We have to explain to them gradually what this withering
away means, and we have begun to do so. . . . Any movement in history which attempts to perpetuate itself becomes
reactionary." His hint to Red bureaucrats: *"Wither away!"*

Tito's world importance, like Stalin's and Mao's, was
made possible by the fact that only three genuine and successful Communist revolutions have taken place in our time
—in the Soviet Union, China and Yugoslavia. All other Communist countries were created by the force of Soviet arms.

Yugoslavia's leader will never be forgotten as the war
hero who saved his country; the national hero who welded

six divergent Balkan peoples into a unified country; the world hero who defied Joseph Stalin and split the Communist world wide open, making independence possible for other Communist nations; the respected elder statesman who brought a better life to his people and who worked for peaceful coexistence between the Communist and Western worlds.

Josip Broz Tito, unique among Communist dictators, is already an impressive legend in his own time.

New York: St. Martin's Press; London: Macmillan & Co., Ltd., 1977.

Suggested Further Readings

Among the dozens of books, magazine articles, and reports read in
research preparation for *Red Rebel*, the following fifteen book titles
have been selected as most likely to reward readers interested in ex-
ploring the subject further:

Archer, Jules. *Man of Steel: Joseph Stalin.* New York: Julian Messner,
1965.

———. *The Dictators.* New York: Hawthorn Books, Inc., Publishers,
1967.

Ayling, S. E. *Portraits of Power.* New York: Barnes & Noble, Inc.,
1964.

Dedijer, Vladimir. *Tito.* New York: Simon & Schuster, 1953.

Djilas, Milovan. *Conversations With Stalin.* New York: Harcourt, Brace
& World, Inc., 1962.

Draskovic, Slobodan M. *Tito: Moscow's Trojan Horse.* Chicago: Henry
Regnery Company, 1957.

Eisenhower, Dwight D. *Mandate For Change.* Garden City, New
York: Doubleday & Company, Inc., 1963.

Fodor, Eugene, ed. *Yugoslavia, 1966.* New York: David McKay Company, Inc., 1966.

Gjupanovic, Dr. Fran. *The Church and State Under Communism. Volume III: Yugoslavia.* Washington, D.C.: U.S. Government Printing
Office, 1965.

Gunther, John. *Procession.* New York, Evanston and London: Harper
& Row, Publishers, 1965.

Hindus, Maurice. *Crisis In the Kremlin.* Garden City, New York:
Doubleday & Company, Inc., 1953.

Maclean, Fitzroy. *The Heretic: Life and Times of Josip Broz-Tito.*
New York: Harper & Row, Publishers, 1957.

McVicker, Charles P. *Titoism: Pattern for International Communism.* New York: St. Martin's Press; London: Macmillan & Co., Ltd., 1957.

Ulam, Adam B. *Titoism and the Cominform.* Cambridge: Harvard University Press, 1946.

White, Leigh. *Balkan Caesar: Tito vs. Stalin.* New York: Charles Scribner's Sons, 1951.

INDEX

Index

About the Author

Jules Archer was born on January 27, 1915, in New York City, attended DeWitt Clinton High School and The City College of New York. He is the author of over a thousand published articles and stories, as well as fourteen books for adults and young people. His work has been translated into twelve languages, reprinted by the State Department, adapted for television and included in anthologies. He has also been a consultant for the World Book Encyclopedia. The Archers live in the foothills of the Taconic Mountain Range at Pine Plains, New York. Their oldest son, Michael, a Princeton graduate, is now a paleontologist in Australia on a Fulbright Scholarship. A second son, Dane, recently graduated from Yale, is a social psychologist. A third son, Kerry, is a high school senior studying for a research career in medical science.